Ro
Villas

The Story of Southfields Grid and its Surroundings

Neil Robson

In partnership with Wandsworth Libraries and Museum

Published by: Neil Robson (020 8874 6341)
Designed by: Arc Design Associates (020 7720 2392)
Printed by: Battley Brothers Limited (020 7622 3401)

ISBN 0 9536467 0 X

1

Acknowledgements

So many people have contributed towards the success of this project, and it is fair to say that without their help this book could not have been written. Valuable suggestions often came from the large number of friends I have made via the Southfields Grid Residents' Association and the Wandsworth Historical Society, but I should like to record my thanks to the following individuals in particular:

Simon Parkinson, former secretary of the SGRA, and John Woodhouse, sometime Chief Librarian at Southfields Library, for their early encouragement when I first started my research

Tony Shaw, former Local History Librarian, for his frequent help and advice

David Emmott, former Vicar of St Barnabas Church, for kindly allowing me access to the *Parish Magazine* files

Keith Bailey, for letting me study his unpublished research on the building of the Grid, and for his constructive criticism of the first two chapters of this book

David Trevor-Jones, for additional information about the Lyceum/Plaza Cinema

Peter Gerhold, for the details about his relative, Spencer Gerhold

Pat Astley-Cooper, Curator at Wandsworth Museum, and Patrick Loobey for their welcome comments at the typescript stage

David Roberts, for designing the finished product

Gordon Pullenger, for his continuing support

and Harold Castle, Eddie King, Edith Robinson and William Skinner for their foresight in writing down their recollections of the Grid in its early years.

But I've saved the best till last. The reminiscences of older residents are still a frequently untapped source for anyone interested in a community's past. For that reason, I am especially grateful to Bob Bolton, May Ellen, Mollie Josey, Joyce Weller and Barbara West who generously gave up their time to discuss their early memories of living in the area. The information and insights that they gave me have proved invaluable.

Picture Credits

All images come from the Wandsworth Local Studies Collection except for the following:

Patrick Loobey (020 8769 0072) - cover, pages 5, 16, 18, 19, 22, 23, 26, 37, 45, 74

St Barnabas Church archive - pages 38, 39, 44

Author's collection - pages 83, 84

2

Contents

(Cover.) Heythorp Street looking south, c. 1906.

(Inside front cover.) Southfields Grid as it appeared on the LCC Municipal Map of London, 1913.

Introduction

"These blasted houses!" roared my friend, arriving late for dinner last summer and keen to apportion the blame. "They all look exactly the same!" I can still recall how protective I felt about the area I have grown to love so well. It was as if I wanted to defend it from attack. Far from taking the view that Southfields Grid is a desert of mediocre sameness, I have come to admire its subtle variety and its ability to soothe the spirit. For here we have a collection of eleven intersecting streets containing just under 2,000 homes, which has managed to generate enormous loyalty and goodwill among its many residents, and offers more of the feel of a charming village than a nondescript inner London suburb.

For a number of years I have wanted to write a celebration of the place that has become my home, focusing on the history of the Grid itself, with added references to the surrounding areas as appropriate; and here at last are the results of those efforts. This is undeniably a potted history; by its nature my account is episodic and certainly contains one or two gaps. But my general approach has been to select a number of key years and treat them as snapshots, capturing the mood of the times and using them to evoke a sense of period. On that basis it is surely not too extravagant to say that this description of one small area within one very large city can easily be appreciated as a glimpse at the life and times of the whole of suburban England over the last century.

There are bound to be a few errors and for these I apologise; and I also hope you will forgive any omission of your school, your own place of worship or your favourite sporting activity. Yet I have deliberately included lots of addresses. If you are a resident on the Grid, and if you see a mention of your own house or that of a friend, I hope you will get a slight thrill of recognition as you read about someone who lived there many years ago.

This is not a story of violent events or exciting conflicts - but then it isn't supposed to be. We choose, when fortune takes a hand, to live in a quiet, comfortable spot, a haven from the cares and worries of the everyday world; and if each month were marked by shootings, fires and general alarms, it might be argued that we are slightly defeating our object.

No, in essence these have been my main aims:

- to prove that even a tranquil, residential suburb can have an interesting past

- to reinforce the feeling of respect for the Grid, founded in part at least on the achievements of the area's previous residents

- to foster a sense of continuity, so that in the years to come people will still be keen to maintain the special atmosphere that our predecessors helped to create.

If I go some way towards achieving those goals, then I can say I will indeed be pleased by the outcome of my efforts.

Neil Robson Heythorp Street, April 2000

A fine impression of Elsenham Street looking south towards Wimbledon Park, c.1906. Vellam House can be clearly seen on the right.

A NOTE ON THE TITLE

By the summer of 1905, the builders had practically finished the Grid and the estate agents in the area were eager to attract people to occupy the few remaining houses. They knew their market - modestly educated families with aspirations to semi-gentility who feared a confined and dull urban existence.

The Wandsworth house agents, Mulliner Brothers, recognised such anxieties and set out to satisfy those longings. Addressing the twin desires for space and rural charm, they hit upon a phrase they knew their clients could not resist. And so it came about that the expression "roomy villas" appeared invitingly in their advertisements at the time.

A NOTE ABOUT PRE-DECIMAL CURRENCY

In 1971, Britain converted to decimal currency. Previously the pound had been divided into 20 shillings, each of them containing 12 pence. The old penny was indicated by the letter "d", a nostalgic throwback to the *denarius* of Roman times, and the shilling by the letter "s" in memory of the Latin *solidus*.

In this book, small amounts are expressed thus: 5d (i.e. fivepence), the equivalent of about 2p. Larger sums are shown like this: 10s 6d (i.e. ten shillings and sixpence), the equivalent of just over 52p. So,

- the 1937 Coronation spoons cost the borough 9d each, which works out at under 4p

- the 8s 6d weekly rent for Mrs Alderton's flat in 1902 comes to about 43p

- the £4 1s 8d spent on Peace decorations at the station in 1919 converts to just over £4.08.

In a nutshell, the old shilling (12 old pence) was the equivalent of five new pence. Maturer readers will scarcely need such reminders. For the younger audience, this must seem like ancient Greek.

Remember though that average wages have increased by a huge amount over the last century, and the real cost of any item in modern terms can be judged only in the context of the typical take-home pay at the time. So things were not always quite as cheap as we might first think.

Little Acorns

Imagine the summer of 1889. While London's dockers struck for a minimum wage of 6d an hour, hundreds of Britons set off for Paris to see Gustave Eiffel's new wrought-iron tower. Book-lovers everywhere were enjoying Jerome K. Jerome's comic account of three men in a boat, just as Gilbert and Sullivan put the finishing touches to their latest operetta, "The Gondoliers". Early on the morning of Monday, 3 June that year, engineers made their final adjustments to a small olive-green locomotive at Wimbledon Station, and shortly after 5.30 the engine steamed slowly out, making its way through Southfields on the first passenger journey up the new railway line to Putney Bridge.

The train halted for a short while at the new station on Wimbledon Park Road, a small well-designed building which had recently been erected in the middle of nowhere. That historic moment defines the starting point for the development of the residential suburb now known as Southfields Grid. People living there today view the area with great pride and affection, but in the eighteen-eighties what would those few early passengers have seen as they looked out of their carriage windows? Fields, farm animals and vegetables - these were the things that would have met their gaze. Southfields was merely a large expanse of meadows at the time, with grazing sheep and extensive market gardens. If they had looked for Replingham Road, they would have sought in vain; it simply did not exist. Its present site was an area of undeveloped grassland and the construction of the new roadway would not be approved for another two years.

Yet if they were well briefed, those travellers would have already been aware that some subtle signs of urban progress were beginning to show. In March 1889 the Wandsworth District Board of Works had to acknowledge that the footpath on Merton Road south of Standen Road was in an unacceptably

DISTRICT & LONDON & SOUTH WESTERN RAILWAYS.

---- *The EXTENSION from* ----

PUTNEY BRIDGE

(FULHAM) TO

WIMBLEDON,

With Intermediate Stations at

East Putney, Southfields, and Wimbledon Park,

WILL OPEN ON

MONDAY, 3RD JUNE, 1889.

See June Time Tables

FOR HALF YEARLY SERVICE OF

Through Trains.

FARES AND SEASON TICKET RATES

TO ALL

DISTRICT RAILWAY STATIONS.

The very beginnings. The Putney and Wandsworth Borough News had to apologise the following week for its "printer's blunder". It inadvertently described the half-hourly service in its advertisement as "half-yearly".

bad state, and as a consequence they were forced to approve the sum of £270 to offset the cost of laying down kerb stones and a covering surface of tar. Another pressing need that year concerned the provision of sufficient school places for the surrounding district. With commendable foresight the Southfields Board School Committee resolved to put up a temporary iron structure pending the completion of a new school on Merton Road precisely where the footpath had been recently improved. That permanent building still stands, now called Riversdale School and a major contributor to the life of Southfields. The carved stone tablets set in its brickwork still proclaim the year of its opening and the surprising fact that in 1890 for educational purposes at least, the area came within the administrative division of Lambeth. Most confident of all of course are the initials of the administrators themselves, the School Board for London.

The railway line itself had taken over two years to construct and cost around £575,000. A trellis-girder bridge was built over the Thames so that the District Railway could join up with the London and South Western Railway and share the other company's stations and tracks. The line emerged from a short tunnel into "one of the prettiest parts of Southfields" according to the opening report, and passed well away from the more expensive mid-Victorian villas on West Hill and Wimbledon Parkside.

Southfields Station itself was destined to become a distinctive focus for the whole surrounding area in years to come. As part of the final preparations that spring, the LSWR proudly carved its own initials in a small shield over the doorway, and early passengers were surprised by the comfortable waiting-room and toilets. Within a month, they had a choice of two services, one direct to Waterloo via East Putney and another to Mansion House via Earls Court. The business strategy of the railway companies was to devote their attention to serving the newer suburban traffic, bringing people living on the south side of the Thames into direct contact with the City and the West End. As a consequence, housing development generally followed along the new lines and that in turn generated greater income, thereby justifying the investment in the first place. However in the light of the slow progress in constructing the Grid, it is far from clear whether the extension from Putney to Wimbledon is a good example of that policy.

Yet for all the gushing promises of the promoters that the railway services would be popular and useful, it has to be said that they were of limited value in the early days. For example, the Mansion House trains ran every half hour at first, which was all that the volume of traffic could justify. Nevertheless the District Railway attempted to increase its turnover by a "tie-in" with a series of late Victorian events which helped to swell the company's coffers. In its initial publicity for the new Wimbledon line for instance, it pushed hard the fact that it could take passengers direct to Earls Court for the 1889 Spanish Exhibition.

The real drawback to early success was the late start-up of the morning train services. Only six trains could be guaranteed to arrive at their destinations before 9 o'clock, limiting their appeal to business men. The journey time to Mansion House took about three-quarters of an hour and it was not exactly cheap. A quarterly season ticket for first-class travel cost £5 10s (which works out at over 1s 8d per day) and a similar ticket for second-class was £3 15s. So-called cheap fares were also available, but the advertisers had no qualms about indicating that these were mainly for workmen.

For all these initial drawbacks however, the new form of transport quickly began to weave its spell. A little way up Wimbledon Park Road, Northampton Villa was put on the market during the first month of passenger trains. It boasted five bedrooms, a bathroom, a splendid entrance hall and a tricycle shed. The agent was seeking a rent of £45 a quarter. To clinch the deal he added a sentence he knew would attract the punters: "Within a few minutes' walk of the Southfields Station in the new line of Railway." The necessary supports for urban expansion were starting to fall neatly into place.

It nevertheless took a few years for that expansion to gain momentum. According to the edition of *Kelly's Directory* compiled in late 1896, there were a mere 32 new buildings in the vicinity of Replingham Road. One of the first arrivals was the builder and decorator, William Castle. He set up in business with his sons on the western corner of Heythorp Street in the premises now occupied by The Grid Inn, public house, and was for many years a dominant figure on the local scene. Another pioneer was a dairyman, William Skinner, who moved into a combined house-and-shop on the opposite corner of Heythorp Street. For the previous 11 years he had been trading in Standen Road following his retirement from the Police Force after 25 years' service.

Another notable building in 1896 was the fine double-fronted Vellam House on the west side of Elsenham Street, and Alfred

Pitts could feel a justified sense of pride when he moved into the place that year. Nor was he alone. To the south of his home, his neighbours were making themselves comfortable in the short terrace of houses called Elsenham Gardens, which the builders had already completed three years earlier.

Otherwise the future Grid was still right on the very fringe of London, with cattle browsing in nearby fields, and the Crystal Palace towering impressively to the east on top of Sydenham Hill. At about this time the novelist and reformer, Walter Besant, gave J. C. Geikie the task of recording the actual condition of every street in south London. There is a hint of dismay in some of his comments on the areas surrounding the station. To the north for example where Granville Road joins Merton Road:

> "small streets of small houses at cheap rents have been pushed into the fields and gardens. The neighbourhood … is dirty and chiefly inhabited by very poor people, for whose benefit rows of tiny shops are established."

Of the Grid where the roads had been defined but house-building had scarcely begun, he noted:

> "Replingham Road…has little knots of dwellings on it. South of Replingham Road a few desultory dwellings scattered over wide spaces follow the laid-out lines of roads running towards (Wimbledon Park)."

July 1902 – possibly the earliest advertisement relating to the Grid. The houses were being renumbered and by the end of the year, Madame Bué was giving her address as 73 Elsenham Street.

Things took off at a staggering pace however with the establishment of an estate agents' office opposite the station in 1899. According to local historian Bernard Rondeau, George Ryan and Henry Penfold were the prime developers at the start of the scheme and they employed builders under contract to construct different sections of the various streets. Their standards were high and they were constantly badgering the contractors about the quality of their work. Socially they were in advance of their time with their option for residents to own or rent their property, a flexible arrangement designed to attract a wide cross-section of different people.

Here are some examples from 1902 to show how that strategy worked in practice. In the summer Mrs

---

MME JULES BUE

(Of Oxford, author of " La Conversation en Classe "),

Teacher of French

(Grammar, Conversation, Literature.)

Private Lessons, Classes, Schools. Lessons by Correspondence.

13, FLORENCE TERRACE, ELSENHAM ST., SOUTHFIELDS, S.W.

Alderton, the baker at the top corner of Astonville Street, advertised her five-room flat at a weekly rent of 8s 6d. At the other end of the scale, an unidentified three-bedroom house near the station was offered for sale at £325, or alternatively at an annual rent of £30. "Suit clerk", added the advertiser cryptically in an attempt to influence the type of tenant he was hoping to get.

By then the new street name-plates were going up, and writing in the nineteen-seventies, Simon Catling thought he had discovered a trend in the origins of at least some of them. Village names appear four times: Brookwood (Surrey), Elsenham (Essex), Lavenham (Suffolk) and Trentham (Staffordshire). Initially the street names were carried south over the borough border into Wimbledon Park, but this arrangement did not survive beyond 1906. In another glimpse of how things might have been, Revelstoke Road (originally planned as Morgan Road) was initially expected to extend west and into the park itself, though mercifully that proposal did not bear fruit.

No pubs were to be included in the area. A strong temperance movement existed in the nineteenth century, and its enthusiastic supporters had no difficulties in making the connection between men having a drink and ignoring their families' needs. As a direct result, when Augusta Beaumont and her family sold the land for development in the eighteen-eighties, a restrictive covenant was included in the deeds of sale which precluded the opening of any public house and this restriction was not resisted for another hundred years.

Travelling by the Underground at the turn of the century was not an undertaking for the faint at heart. Women frequently carried a duster with them and it was common for many travellers to put down an old newspaper before settling into their seat. Belching out smoke and soot, the District Railway engines were strange-looking contraptions, with huge pipes down the sides of the boiler which were supposed to reduce the steam in the tunnels further up the line and convert it back into water.

The four-wheel carriages had a curious appearance too. They were very short, measuring less than 27 feet in length, and their bodies were made of varnished teak. Passengers who bought first-class tickets sat in reasonable, upholstered comfort, but the second-class compartments were rather more basic and cramped. Third-class travellers had to make do with a bench covered with a strip of carpet. Nobody expected heating which was fortunate as none was provided; and at night or in winter it was not always easy to read as the gas lighting fuelled by cylinders of compressed oil-gas became progressively dimmer. Furthermore, it was tough if someone wanted to travel on a Sunday morning since the service was routinely suspended between 11 am and 1 pm. Known as the "church interval", this disruption was considered to be totally reasonable and lasted until July 1903.

There were other inconveniences in those early years, especially before the street surfaces were properly made up. One of the first residents recalled that they were a mixture of sand and gravel, regularly churned up by the handcarts and horse-drawn traffic. Nearly £800 was raised in rates in one year from Elsenham Street alone, and yet the rate-payers felt they got nothing in return except days of mud when it rained and clouds of dust in dry weather, a situation that called for frequent visits from the council steam-roller.

Matters came to a head in September 1902. The New Streets Committee of Wandsworth Borough Council decided that the work of surfacing the roadway should be carried out under the direction of the district surveyor, and that each household should make a contribution to the cost. This proposal infuriated a group of local residents, many of them living on modest means and coping with the inevitable expense of moving into a new area. They could see no justification in laying down an expensive form of concrete surface without any discussion, despite the reassurances that it would allegedly look better in 30 years' time. One of the prime objectors at a public meeting was William McBirney of 94 Elsenham Street who declared amid much merriment that he saw no reason why Southfields should be paved with "fancy marble, with gold trimmings". A Mr Haird claimed that he had 40 years' experience in the business and therefore had some knowledge on the subject. The council intended to charge each house £1 12s per foot, whereas an independent contractor could do it cheaper at a rate of £1 6s 6d, he said.

Acrimonious exchanges followed between the deputation and the council. Eventually the councillors backed down; outside contractors were involved and the lowest tender for paving with tar was accepted. This challenge of authority can be seen as something of a test case. Here was an expanding population of ratepayers. The essential services like a few lamp-posts were slow to appear, and even then their arrival seemed to be little more than a superficial gesture. By taking their stand, they proved a need for sensitivity towards the feelings of local residents, a consideration which still holds true to this day.

Before we leave that particular winter, we should note that William McBirney appeared in the papers a second time. In December 1902, burglars made their way into 98 Elsenham Street while Reginald Medley and his wife were out and stole silver plate, some jewellery and an amount of cash. In a precursor to Neighbourhood Watch, Mr McBirney saw the thieves and gave chase but without success. So with sadness we must face the truth that quiet, south London suburbs were not free from crime, even in Edwardian times.

All was not gloom however, and those early years brought much for the newcomers to celebrate. The Coronation of King Edward VII for example was destined to be a major royal event. The date of the ceremony was set for Thursday, 26 June 1902, and preparations were well advanced for a children's fete to be held in Southfields on the Wednesday of the following week. The site had been chosen: Leg of Mutton field, which covered the area now occupied by Skeena Hill, and was so called because of its shape. The borough council had turned down a request for a grant of £50 to erect a decorative arch at the entrance and instead, true to form, it asked all businesses to decorate their premises themselves in an appropriate manner.

However King Edward developed appendicitis (or perityphlitis, as the doctors called it at the time). The news of his illness was announced in London at noon on Tuesday the 24th and reached Wandsworth in under an hour-and-a-half. Consternation followed, though it was soon dispelled by the royal request that all civic celebrations should continue unchanged.

In any case these were supplemented by a number of quite independent, private events. One such took place on the Grid's own doorstep. George Gale was one of the main builders in the area and he lived on Wimbledon Park Road in the house then known as 13 Gloucester Terrace, just south of Standen Road. He owned the adjacent field (situated to the north of the present Southfields Baptist Church building) and it was there that he had invited 300 local children to a party on the original Coronation Day itself. The event went ahead as planned, and he was assisted for the most part by members of the local Baptist Church, which was then on Merton Road at the northern corner of Standen Road. Each child was given a souvenir mug and was served what was described as a "cold collation". Mr Gale laid on entertainments, the most memorable being a minstrel troupe made up of employees from Price's candle factory, appearing under a name acceptable at the time: "The Florida Coons".

However the official local event was yet to come, and the weather on 2 July was beautiful. The children assembled in Wandsworth High Street at 12.45 and marched for about an hour behind their own school's banner down Buckhold Road and across to the site of the fete on the western side of the railway line. Transport for the children was simply not considered. The procession was accompanied by three bands, a truly local connection being made by the inclusion of the London & South Western Railway Servants' Band who were hired for £1.

By some stroke of good fortune, a reporter from the *Wandsworth Borough News* captured the still-rural nature of the area with this enchanting account:

> "A gay and attractive scene met the gaze of the youthful guests when they arrived at their destination at 2 o'clock. The acres of pasture-land were looking their very best, the tall and stately trees were in their full summer beauty, and, but for the noise of frequent trains passing near by, and the sight of a few tall factory chimneys in the distance, the little ones might have imagined that they were in the very heart of the country."

A total of over 12,000 people attended, and they were treated to steam roundabouts, Punch and Judy, minstrels and - to use the style of those neo-Edwardians - "cocoa-nut shies". They stood open mouthed as they watched the main attraction, Lady Hercules, whose chief feat was lifting a horse off the ground. Tea was available for the children from 3.30, served in the obligatory commemorative mug; and before the afternoon was over, Novello's, the music publishers, gave each child a free copy of "Now Pray We For Our Country", a ditty sadly lost to us with the passing of time.

To general great relief, the King survived the distinct risks associated with his operation and he was duly crowned in Westminster Abbey on 9 August. That notable summer provided us with an exceptional legacy which has already lasted a hundred years. The Mayor of Wandsworth in 1901-2 was Sir William Lancaster, a larger-than-life character and subsequently grandfather of the cartoonist, Sir Osbert Lancaster. There was a piggery and fat-boiling works at the eastern ends of Replingham and Pirbright Roads, and its situation was particularly obnoxious once the new Merton Road School had been established. On 25 May 1902, Sir William announced to the council with great flourish that he had purchased the two acres of land and proposed that they be laid out as a recreation ground for young people with seats for the elderly. His vision became a reality in the form of Coronation Gardens. He added archly that his two sisters "who seem to have a very high opinion of the mayor" intended to have a drinking fountain erected in memory of their brother's term of office.

Their beneficence does indeed still remain, a monolith of granite bordered by a rather sad and bent railing, and still supporting a basin in the Arts and Crafts style decorated with a couple of little water-lilies. The figure of Aquarius has sadly long since been removed. Nevertheless Sir William's great generosity has survived in the form of an amenity for the whole area. A comparison with an early photograph may reveal that the railings surrounding the grass have gone and a large central pavilion has also disappeared. Yet the smaller stand and the sheer benefit of a bit of open space still remain; for which forethought we may say many thanks.

Taller Oaks

By the autumn of 1903 Replingham Road was effectively completed, but since its construction had progressed in such a piecemeal fashion, the house numbering was amazingly haphazard and incoherent. The numbers on the north side ran smoothly enough, but on the south they started at both ends. There were five No 1's and two Station Parades. Various terraces were given distinctive names such as Belgrave, Grosvenor and Rywell, though these were inevitably abandoned with the need to sort the addresses into a more logical order. In an expanding London, Edwardian householders had to reconcile themselves to the problems of renumbering, much as we must cope with regular updates to our dialling codes.

An early shot of Replingham Road, c.1907, with The World's Stores grocery chain newly established at No. 4. The tiles on either side of Morrison and Fleet's dairy at No. 10 were blue and white.

At that same time, late 1903, the Grid was practically complete down to a line that included Lavenham Road. Only a few gaps remained to be filled during the next two years, the largest being a space on the western side of the middle section of

Replingham Road.

Engadine Street. In that same period, the remaining area down to the borough boundary was covered by the longer, southern-most blocks and these have a very different feel to them. They are altogether more regular, and each of their lengthy terraces was generally built along a more uniform pattern.

It helps to know why the Grid was so appealing in the first place. The development was an outstanding success from the start mainly because it coincided with the evolution of a new type of city-dweller. The much improved education system of the later Victorian era produced families with a clerk, civil servant or shopkeeper at the head, people whose taste was being moulded by popular novels and monthly magazines. They feared the drab routine and colourless monotony of city life, and the developers enticed them out to the suburbs with houses that were spacious and attractively designed. Their care over detail and the need to appeal is just as enticing today, and modern visitors can still enjoy the delights of the leaded-glass front doors and the attractive tiles in many of the porches. Outstanding examples of the latter - little gems of the Arts and Crafts Movement - can be seen in particular at the northern end of Clonmore Street. Among other highspots are the houses that a Mr Merredew built in the top left-hand block of Engadine Street during 1902. As if to leave his special mark on the whole area, he commissioned a design to be admired: fine, tall windows, cast-iron trim over the porches and elaborately moulded pediments in the gables to the roofs.

Here are some examples which reflect the property prices of the period. In Lavenham Road in 1905, the "compact villa residence" at No 114 was offered on a 99 year lease for £290, and around the same time the shorter-term lease for No 141 was available at £3 3s per month. In 1906 Walter Clist, the newsagent, was paying a mere £47 a year for the rent of his new corner shop at 106 Brookwood Road, just as Jonathan Caley was struggling to establish his greengrocery business on the corner site at 106 Lavenham Road. His 99 year lease set him back £400. In 1909 Thomas Winter took up the offer of three rooms at 80 Elborough Street for 8s per week, lured by the advertiser's reassurance that it was a select neighbourhood. Presumably he had no children, because it was made quite clear in the paper that he would be turned away if he had.

An expanding area demanded better public transport, and in the autumn of 1905, the Wandsworth Traders' Association approached both Thomas Tilling & Co. (who were famous for their fleets of hansom cabs and horse-drawn buses) and the

The Station, Southfields

Fuller's, PhotoSeries

Southfields Station photographed on a hot day, c. 1904. Steam from a passing train drifts above the low wall and the pedestrian on the right pauses to wipe the perspiration from his brow. The object to the left of the broom is a public fire-alarm.

Arrow Co. to see if either could run a bus service between Wandsworth town centre and Southfields. Both operators pleaded difficulties in finding a suitable route, the hilly nature of the area proving more than a match for the limited strength of their motor-buses at the time. An incident in April 1908 does nevertheless show that some form of service was being provided, making use of a more established technology. A Star omnibus had left the station and was travelling down Replingham Road when the horse bolted at the top of Engadine Street knocking down a lamppost and two low walls. The driver was badly injured and a lady passenger later complained that she had been bruised and very shaken. For her at least the new-style motor-buses could not come a moment too soon.

The railway service saw substantial improvements when the District Railway introduced electric trains from 28 August 1905. At a stroke journey times were cut by a quarter, which meant that many more trains could run along the two routes. The expansion of the services was considerable and by the summer of 1914, over 130 trains ran through Southfields Station each day. The new form of traction meant new rolling-stock and the effect was staggering. Gone was the repellent grime of the old carriages. In their place were American-style cars with flat-fronted driving cabs, clerestory roofs and sliding doors. Wandsworth caught a glimpse of Chicago and it liked what it saw.

The other form of transport making an impact at the time was air travel or more precisely, lighter-than-air machines. Every attempt at human progress brings with it great risks, and some are bound to end in tragedy. One such disaster occurred at the Franco-British Exhibition at Shepherd's Bush in August 1908 and resulted in calamity for two of the residents on the Grid.

An airship display had been planned as one of the many exciting features at the exhibition, not only for the visitors' enjoyment but for their education, and George Waites who lived at 137 Elsenham Street was employed to give lectures on aeronautics. On the fateful day he was accompanied by a neighbour, John Leonard of 46 Elborough Street, and together with others they set to work making repairs to the airship and preparing for the demonstration flight.

Suddenly there was a terrific explosion and the noise was heard over the entire exhibition site. Five people suffered terrible injuries; John Leonard received appalling burns to his face and hands, and the condition of George Waites was so serious that he died within a short time in Hammersmith Infirmary. As part of the process of inflating the airship, an electric fan had been used to force hydrogen into the gas-bag, and the jury held the view at the inquest that the accident was caused by a spark

Brookwood Road looking east on a sunny afternoon, c. 1910. A barber's pole identifies Frederick Matthews' hairdressing business at No. 46.

19

from the fan itself as it was being switched off.

The deaths and suffering seem so futile now, yet at the time they helped to advance this particular field of technical knowledge. As the coroner said,

> "At this stage in civilisation, when so much attention is being directed to airships, it becomes very important that (we) should, if possible, be able to locate all known sources of danger."

The contribution of Mr Waites and Mr Leonard is typical of the risks that so many are willing to take in order that man can make progress.

Excited crowds gather at the corner of Trentham Street in May 1911 to watch as a balloon is untangled from the roofs of two houses in Brookwood Road.

Airships may still have been rare, but balloons were a much more frequent sight over south London prior to the start of the First World War. On a fine Saturday afternoon, it was common to see a dozen or more in the sky at one time, all of them at the mercy of any changes in the weather. Up would spring a thunderstorm and many of the balloonists were forced to make a rapid descent into people's back gardens or the roadway below them. One such well publicised incident occurred in May 1911.

A party of five led by an officer of the Grenadier Guards set off from Wimbledon on the afternoon of the 6th and the wind carried them in the direction of Wandsworth. As they were passing over Southfields, the balloon lost height, hit some telegraph wires and crashed on top of Mrs Goddard's stationery shop at 70 Brookwood Road. People started to gather and the balloonists threw down some guide ropes. One of these was grasped by a man standing on the pavement. At that moment there was a sudden gust of wind and the balloon shot up, jerking him off the ground. He decided to hold on, and enjoyed the relaxing experience of being hauled high onto the rooftops. He slid down the rope fortunately uninjured, and the balloon drifted further along the street dislodging chimney pots and roof tiles. Brickwork tumbled into the road narrowly missing the crowd of spectators, by now a sea of boaters, flat caps and cartwheel hats.

Eventually some of the men were able to seize the ropes and drag the basket down, the balloon itself settling as a tangled mass on the roof of Henry Fry's house at No 102. The captain's party stepped out a trifle unnerved but otherwise unharmed. They pulled the valve cord to let the gas escape, packed the balloon in its basket and waited for a wagon to take away the now impotent contraption. The incident was over and all was well again; but there can have been few homes that blustery weekend where it was not the main topic of tea-time conversation.

Two major local events in the Edwardian decade stand out above all others: a royal visit and a religious ceremony of great significance. In Coronation year royalty was admired from afar; by 1905 it could be inspected at rather closer quarters. On 13 July that year, the Southfields Children's Flower Show and Fete was held in the field to the north of the station on the eastern side of the track, and Princess Christian of Schleswig-Holstein agreed to attend in the role of its patron. Originally christened Helena, Princess Christian was one of Queen Victoria's many daughters. A popular character, she was aged 59 at the time and renowned for her many good works.

It was beautifully sunny that floral Thursday, and the cultivated pot-plants and specimens grown from seed were displayed in a large marquee where they were considered by the *Wandsworth Borough News* to be "of pretty universal excellence". The local residents demonstrated their patriotic enthusiasm by "decorating their dwellings in a becomingly gay fashion". Flags and bunting were stretched across the junction at the top of Replingham Road, and the developers Ryan and

Replingham Road ready for Princess Christian's visit in July 1905. Note the undeveloped site for the London City and Midland Bank on the left.

Penfold suspended Chinese lanterns from the eaves of their office opposite the station.

By 3.30 the official party had assembled to greet their visitor. They included the mayor and mayoress, who that year were the Rev. Alderman and Mrs Anderson, several members of the borough council in their state robes and the local MP, Sir Henry Kimber. Some insight into Princess Christian's dress sense can be gained from the fact that she wore a gown of grey silk trimmed with white, and topped it with a mauve toque.

Sir Henry gushed that she had brought royal weather with her, and the mayor found it extremely gratifying that she should have favoured such an occasion with her gracious presence. Her Royal Highness conserved her energy by distributing the first prizes only and making no speech, though she "bowed her acknowledgements" to the various votes of thanks. She did however tour the tent for some time examining the exhibits in great detail, and the sight of her gave considerable pleasure to the large numbers of people who were drawn by the prospect of seeing a member of the royal family at close hand.

She watched a maypole dance by 12 little girls,

"prettily attired…(in) white frocks and yellow and green sashes, while in their hair they had wreaths of smilax and marguerites".

The performance proved so successful that it was repeated once the royal party had left. And so the day drew to its close with races for the children, variety entertainment from the Elysian Pierrots and lively music from the grandly named 4th Volunteer Brigade East Surrey Regimental Band.

For the other major event, 9 May 1908 was selected as the day to celebrate the consecration of St Barnabas Church and there was intense excitement amongst the many parishioners as they looked forward to the ceremony itself. The dedication stone had been laid 18 months earlier in November 1906 in response to the pressing need for larger premises. The original mission church, north of Burr Road, was constructed out of iron and held a mere 200. The population of the district in 1904 was already over 9,000, and by 1907 it exceeded 13,000. The vast majority of the residents were Christian, and many were Anglican. Roman Catholics would still have to travel to worship, but a large new building for members of the Church of England with a seating capacity of 800 could easily be justified.

The first occupants move into the southern end of Elsenham Street in 1906 and make full use of the Venetian blinds fitted as standard by the developer. Already the weeds in the roadway are crying out for attention The houses nearest to the camera were destroyed by bombing in 1940.

The commission went to the architect C. Ford Whitcombe and his design was a free adaptation of the late fourteenth century English Gothic style, based on many of the churches he had seen in East Anglia. He wanted to give an impression of airiness inside, and his optimistic intentions can be judged by the way the church's proportions allow the eye to soar. The feeling of height is rather stronger than the one of breadth.

The appeals for donations were intense, but despite many generous gifts of furnishings and plate, the target of £10,000 was never achieved. Put simply, the aims were already outdated and the church therefore falls neatly into that category of suburban imitation-mediaeval buildings so accurately defined by John Betjeman. Shortage of funds meant that the planned tower over the Lavenham Road entrance was never built, and the church opened with a totally inadequate organ. Yet in many respects the modern visitor has reaped a definite benefit from this unavoidable austerity. We can enjoy an impressive building of a size that would be inconceivable today. Instead of a fussy over-decorated interior, one solitary pillar carries any mouldings. The simple "temporary" glazing is a bonus too. Rather than an expanse of multi-coloured glass, we are treated to windows of muted olive-green or amber which look curiously pleasing in bright sunlight.

Back to that momentous Saturday. By 3.15 the vast church was filled to capacity and the ticket-only congregation waited with mounting tension as the choirs set out from the old "tin" church singing with great gusto "Onward Christian Soldiers" and other stirring hymns. For those in the new church a particularly memorable feature was the impression made by the rising sound of many voices, as the long procession drew gradually nearer down Merton Road.

Finally the Bishop of Southwark arrived at the main entrance and striking the door with his staff gained admission to perform the ceremony of consecration. His sermon made reference to the fact that St Barnabas Church was part of an adjacent parish and he neatly summarised the impact of the recent staggering changes to the area:

> "Southfields has grown up...almost with mushroom growth, part of that quiet refined parish of St Paul's, Wimbledon Park, and yet not part of it. Sometimes people...were inclined to say, "Who are these newcomers? We don't know them: we wish they had kept away: we have no concern with them." (Others) had looked down the hill

upon those whose dwellings were springing up beneath them, and said, "We must do something for these people.""

So, how were "these people" bringing some order to their new lives? One clear trend in an era of fewer controls and regulations was the establishment of miniature schools and colleges. Miss Gertrude Thompson appointed herself as principal of Clonmore House School at 178 Clonmore Street where she taught piano-playing among a number of other subjects. Florence Poggio set up her grandly named Southfields College at 61 and 63 Elborough Street; and further down at No 123, Mrs Drake and her daughters opened a Modern School for girls and boys in September 1908 where they offered to prepare their pupils for Oxford and Cambridge exams.

No sooner had the Grid been built, with gas as the dominant energy source, than the electricity suppliers made concerted efforts to convert potential customers to their own product. Leading the field, the County of London Electric Supply Co. Ltd offered to wire houses and charge on the quarterly rental or slot meter systems. As a further enticement, their prices started to tumble. The cost of a unit was reduced in October 1905 from 6d to fivepence-ha'penny, and by the end of the decade it had fallen to a staggering three-halfpence, mainly in order to popularise the use of electricity for heating and cooking.

A selection of minor events and trivia provides an intriguing insight into day-to-day life in Edwardian Southfields. Financial worries, for example, are no respecters of location, and poor Claire Parker of 43 Replingham Road found herself declared bankrupt in the middle of the decade. She titled herself a professor of dancing and deportment, and had been in her line of business since 1876.

Three thieves broke into Lillie Yeatman's furniture shop at 91 Replingham Road in August 1905 and stole £20 worth of gold jewellery. Punishment was severe. The ring-leader was sentenced to nine months' hard labour because of a previous conviction. The other two received shorter terms of imprisonment and, as if to fulfil some moral fable, they both expressed a willingness to go abroad when they were released, though with what enthusiasm is far from clear.

In a strongly Conservative area, Harry Dubery of 40 Lavenham Road stoutly battled on behalf of the Wandsworth Independent Labour Party despite the sarcastic attacks of his political foes. But it was an uphill struggle for him; in a council by-election in December 1907 he polled a mere 247 votes.

Austin, Willis & Co. conducted their drapery business from this vast site until about 1923. This scene, c. 1908, illustrates the firm's philosophy that it was not possible to overfill a display window.

In June 1908 a ferocious storm broke over the area and 38 Heythorp Street was struck by lightning. In an account that might raise more mirth than is strictly kind, we are told that a bed-ridden old lady lay helpless in a room beneath the smoking remains of the shattered chimney.

Finally a story from the autumn of that same year shows how tough obtaining a divorce used to be. Amelia Dunn of 114 Clonmore Street alleged that her husband Matthew had deserted her. The Police Court magistrate was not convinced and told her to bring proceedings for the restitution of conjugal rights. In other words, "Go and get him back!" It was "a wife's dilemma", as the *Wandsworth Borough News* reporter tartly put it.

If we had had an opportunity to walk around the streets in the months leading up to the First World War, what would have struck us as distinctive or strange? The houses would have looked more drab than nowadays, with a dull uniformity as yet unaffected by alterations and repairs. The paintwork then was generally darker than now, though the new sash widows could easily be flung way up high in warm weather. The low front walls with their filigree cast-iron railings generally drew the eye along without variation, and saplings rather than sturdy trees lined the roads which were totally empty of cars.

Up at the station on quieter days, the porters would lean on their barrows waiting to help the next train-load of passengers upon their arrival. Small corner shops abounded, and approximately 50 businesses were established in Replingham Road alone. Virtually all were given over to a specific trade: sweetshops, drapers, grocers, dairies, ironmongers, laundries. Mrs Spells baked on the premises at No 8 and sold the previous day's cakes at 13 for a shilling. People went to Mr Bate the oilman at No 12 for their candles and gas mantles, and then they might cross over to Alfred Bridges' music shop at No 15 to admire his window display of a double bass and a violin tastefully positioned on a chair.

The suburb could even sustain Thomas Seldon's corn merchant business at No 25. He had many customers who needed animal food for their delivery horses or other agricultural purposes. After all, cows were kept a mere half mile away at 9 Revelstoke Road, the site of E. Manley's Wimbledon Park Farm.

The continuing dependence on animals even in a residential area was still very strong. A large grey granite horse-trough was situated in front of the station, originally for the benefit of the late-Victorian horse-cabs, and a pink stone drinking fountain stood outside the Midland Bank, complete with four metal cups attached by chains. It even had a small, low-level trough to provide water for dogs.

Nevertheless it cannot be over-emphasised that Southfields Grid stood on the very brink of built-up London. Children played in the grassland at the end of Gartmoor Gardens and wandered along Sutherland Grove, a mere cinder path where the trees met overhead. There they would pick handfuls of bluebells and fill their bowls with brambles when they were ripe and juicy.

In July 1912, barely two years before the fateful summer of 1914, the *Daily Chronicle* asked its readers for the whereabouts of the closest haystacks to the middle of London and the answer that came back was: Southfields. One correspondent in particular filled her letter with gushing rustic charm, describing how she had left the station a few days earlier and seen sunburnt men labouring to cut the hay, the air heavy with the scent of the stuff. She ended by saying, "One fancies that Arcadia's edge is where the lamp-posts stop and the haystacks begin." Sad to say Arcadia's days were already distinctly numbered.

The Impact Of War

In their time the two world wars of the twentieth century produced a markedly different response from the people on the home front. The second conflict was truly seen as a citizen's war involving everyone with a great intensity; but World War One, at least in the earlier stages, was viewed as a decidedly more distant affair. For sure, if your husband or son went off to fight for King and Country, the trauma affected you for the rest of your life; but for the majority of other Londoners, the impact of the war amounted to little more than a dire catalogue of sombre casualty lists, rationing, general shortage of familiar things and the terror caused by the occasional Zeppelin passing overhead. Nevertheless this sense of detachment did not dispel the general feeling amongst the men at home that they must show their support for the struggle by enthusiastically taking part in some form of worthy action.

By the beginning of 1915 a patriotic group of Southfields residents had banded together to form a volunteer army to protect their homes and families. Calling themselves the Southfields Defence Force, this forerunner of the Home Guard included two headmasters from Merton Road, Tom Hendra the postmaster on Revelstoke Road, and William Castle, the builder who had been one of the area's first residents at 22 Replingham Road. Initially their office was part of the London County and Westminster Bank at 2 Replingham Road and, in an earnest form of displacement therapy, their early efforts consisted of nothing more than practising to march smartly and attending church parades.

Yet they were not alone; and the government, recognising the value of these many volunteer forces and the need to co-ordinate their efforts, set up the County of London Volunteer Regiment. The temporary armbands and dummy rifles gave way to proper arms and ammunition; and a distinctive uniform was designed in green which in Southfields could be bought from Austin, Willis & Co., the large drapery store at 24-8 Replingham Road.

Now that they were renamed the 13th Battalion of that regiment, the men were required to channel their energies towards more practical activities. At the local miniature rifle

JAM FROM AUSTRALIA

We have purchased the entire shipment Ex. the Steamship 'KHIVA' & now offer at prices fixed by

THE FOOD CONTROLLER

APPLE JELLY	1/4
BLACK CURRANT	1/8½
BLACKBERRY	1/5½
MELON & LEMON	1/7
PEACH	1/7½
PLUM	1/3½
RASPBERRY	1/7½

PER 27 OZ. TIN.

TWICE as sweet as ordinary Jam

WORLD'S STORES

Pioneers of Popular Prices

4, Replingham Road, Southfields, S.W.

These First World War advertisements were designed for The World's Stores in a central studio and simply modified for local branch needs. Despite official campaigns urging people to economise, the government's food controller, Lord Rhondda, eventually had to introduce rationing in the October of 1917.

This is what you want for

MEATLESS DAYS

CHEAP FOOD

BEST PINK
SALMON 9d.
Large Tall Tin

SALMON CUTLET 6½d.
Half Flat Tins

WORLD'S STORES

Pioneers of Popular Prices

4, Replingham Road, Southfields, S.W.

range they learnt to shoot straight, and they also dug trenches on Wimbledon Common. Enemy invasion was a distinct possibility and, to combat this threat, younger members were trained as cycle-messengers. Their efforts increased and by the summer of 1916, a regular Sunday morning sight was the convoy of army lorries leaving Southfields Station to carry officers and men on a day's trench digging near Biggin Hill.

These defence preparations were treated with a deadly seriousness which remained constant right through to the final months of the war. For years on end there was little comfort in the war news, and as late as the spring of 1918, defeat was still seen as a very real possibility. If the German's last "big push" had been more successful, the remains of the regular army based in Britain would have been ordered over to France and all of the volunteer battalions would have been on active service. Many wives and daughters held their breath at the thought of what those implications might hold for them.

Month after month these same people avidly scanned the *St Barnabas Church Magazine*, trying to comprehend the grim Roll of Honour in each issue and come to terms with the columns of letters from members of the parish away with the forces. Here are three examples from the autumn of 1916:

> Corporal F. Earp: Please thank those who are responsible for the sending to me of the church Magazine…I think it fetches one as near home as anything I know of.

> Seaman C. Robinson: The copy for April…was taking passage in the ill-fated S.S. "Sussex," and bore the mark "Damaged by immersion in water," though after having travelled some 3,000 miles, reached me in excellent condition.

> Private H. Martyn: I am…assisting at the dressing station, and it is very pitiful at times to see the poor fellows come in, with mud and - (half page torn away by Censor).

In their grief one family erected a memorial plaque in the church to their fallen loved one. Arthur Rhodes was serving with the Seaforth Highlanders and was killed in November 1916 while carrying despatches on the Somme. He had lived at 6 Engadine Street and had been a chorister and server at the church where they described him as "a splendid type of manly Christian." He was only 20.

In the same month Lieutenant James Pulleyn of the Royal Flying Corps also died at the front. He had lived with his family at 85 Elsenham Street and had been a Sunday School teacher before the war. He was shot down while flying over the trenches, but in a final twist that filled his neighbours with horror, the enemy opened fire on him a second time and killed him before his machine hit the ground.

The court cases from that same wretched year reflect the mood of the times. The Military Service Tribunal sat daily, hearing a stream of pleas for exemption and generally rejecting them with what to us seems like a cruel level of intolerance. To generate an even greater sense of shame and guilt the Recruiting Officer of Wandsworth published long weekly lists of names in the papers, asking for information on whether those mentioned had joined up, had moved away or were known to be exempt. Against this background the mayor, Alderman Archibald Dawnay, heard the defence of one particular Southfields tradesman in 1916, unnamed in the published reports to avoid embarrassment or retribution if he were granted exemption. The shopkeeper claimed he was purchasing his business by monthly instalments, and he would have to close down if he were called up, throwing several assistants out of work. The tribunal gave him a delay of two months in which to find someone to take over the temporary running of his shop until he returned from the fighting "as a general!", as the good alderman put it with a certain leaden jocularity.

The courts had no qualms about imposing harsh punishments whenever they could. Tight licensing laws were brought in to maintain the productivity levels of the country's munitions workers and Edward Collinson, who ran the off-licence at 1 Replingham Road, escaped conviction for selling alcohol out of hours only because of the lack of evidence.

Less fortunate was Christopher Verbunas, a tailor's cutter living in Lavenham Road, who was registered as a German subject. He failed to tell the police that he had moved and was given the choice of a £25 fine or two months' imprisonment.

Strict blackout restrictions were imposed and no-one could expect mercy from the magistrates. In October 1916 the *Wandsworth Borough News* carried a paragraph reporting that George Barrett of 69 Lavenham Road had been fined £3 for not screening a light. Before the end of the year Montague Smith of 38 Elsenham Street was charged with the same offence. He pleaded that he had gone to bed and forgotten, but he was still made to pay a fine of £2.

The Lyceum Cinema finally opens its doors in 1917. The high top-price for the reserved seats defines the event as a major effort at fund raising.

Fortunately there were still some pastimes to help people at home take their minds off their many woes. They could, for example, put their gardening skills to full effect. The Southfields Agriculture (War) Committee was set up, all vacant land including Wimbledon Park was taken over, and amateur gardeners set to work producing vegetables and large quantities of soft fruit for jam making, an effort that anticipated the Dig for Victory campaign by some 25 years.

Another event to ease the gloom, one with far reaching consequences, was the opening of the Lyceum Cinema on Wimbledon Park Road. Plans had been approved as far back as November 1915, but development was twice delayed by the Minister of Munitions. Eventually the building was completed and on Saturday, 27 January 1917 the Volunteer Battalion formed a guard of honour to greet the arrival of the mayor, Alderman and Mrs Dawnay. They were welcomed by the manager, Albert Harwood, and found a hall that could seat an audience of 1250 people, fitted with a reasonably sized screen which measured 24 feet by 18 feet. From the technical standpoint, the projection equipment was at the cutting edge. "The most up-to-date and complete bioscope machines on the market have been installed to ensure a good picture," the *Wandsworth Borough News* informed its readers.

The building is now the site of Jesters Snooker Club and still merits an intriguing, short visit. By some happy chance the fine barrel-vaulted ceiling has survived basically intact, and the moulded wreathes and garlands decorating the inside walls are now attractively picked out in a range of different colours.

As a form of entertainment in its early years, the cinema had acquired a reputation for promoting immorality and corrupting the values of the young. But the tide was starting to turn, and the mayor picked up on this shift of opinion in his opening speech. What pictures he had seen he had greatly enjoyed, he said, and he was sure that the management would show only high quality films which would amuse, educate and instruct. "No mother need fear to bring her daughter, and no father his son," he reassured his audience.

The first day was a charity event and half of the proceeds went to Roehampton Hospital, with the remainder being handed to the Volunteer Battalion. By now 500 strong they were warmly praised for their efforts by Alderman Dawnay, though he hit the Dad's Army pathos of a future generation when he remarked to loud applause, "If the Germans ever came to Southfields, very few of them would ever get back again." Fortunately such wishful thinking was never put to the test.

The films that followed his speech were enthusiastically received, but the account of the event mentions only one of them in any detail, a documentary about the Somme offensive entitled "The Battle of the Ancre", which showed tanks going into action and clearing all obstacles from their paths. A local journalist enthused:

> "It was an inspiring sight to see these land monsters ambling unconcernedly towards the enemy lines, and the picture will live long in the memories of all who saw it."

With audiences numbed by the unending death-toll, the strain of the air-raids and increasingly tight food controls, it is hardly surprising that he should express such a fascination for that particularly fiendish item of warfare.

The reporter's hard-heartedness and the general feeling of doom is still easy to understand. Within months Gotha war-planes were flying over south London, dropping their bombs on Putney Common and Tooting, which was far too close for comfort. Peace still seemed unattainable and the country was driven to the very brink of despair by the fear that the war would never come to an end. Eventually the new year of 1918 arrived and further viscious fighting ensued. Finally the Great Powers ran out of men to throw at each other for slaughter and, exhausted, they mercifully agreed to an armistice on the morning of 11 November.

A Grid Fit For Heroes

We would have seen few men on the Grid at the start of 1919. The symbol of an "absent voter" appears against many a male name on the electoral register, and large numbers of troops were waiting demobilisation and their journey home from northern France. Over a hundred former residents had been killed, many more were wounded; and yet there was a general mood of upbeat cheerfulness in the air. Against a picture of a happy family, wreathed in smiles and sitting round a groaning table, The World's Stores at 4 Replingham Road promised "Peace and Contentment" to those who chose to eat the wholesome foods they offered in their shop.

By the late spring, the government had declared Saturday, 19 July a national day of celebration, and the Southfields Peace Committee quickly started their task of designing a suitable programme for festivities. They secured the grounds of the Wimbledon Park Golf Club for a Grand Carnival and drew up the plans for a procession which would pull together the many differing local interests.

Let us first take stock of the social scene that poignant summer, for there were a number of anxieties and concerns to concentrate the collective mind. Profiteering was a big worry, and local traders went to great pains to demonstrate their sensitivity towards general criticism about the amounts that were being charged. "Bargains at pre-war prices!", declared The World's Stores, whilst a writer to the papers was exceptionally irritated by the increasing cost of a ball of wool. A campaign to raise money to provide milk for German babies led to some angry exchanges and an indication that forgiveness would be many years in the future. The indignation of certain returning soldiers also went into overdrive. During the air-raids towards the end of the war, boy scouts had toured the streets sounding the "all clear" on their bugles. For this public-spirited activity they were each to receive a bronze medal, an indefensible indulgence in the eyes of many of the servicemen.

There were a reasonable number of jobs to be had, particularly for youngsters looking for work, and in the days before our own equal opportunities sensitivities, Fuller's Library at 27 Replingham Road had no qualms about asking for "a girl just leaving school". In the same spirit, Harry Horden felt no guilts about specifically advertising for a lad to work in his fried fish shop at 58 Brookwood Road. Another small-ad lets us peep into that era. In the garden of 80 Heythorp Street, Alfred Allen kept white leghorn cockerels, and he offered seven of them for sale at 7s 6d each. Undoubtedly the sounds and the smells were a pleasant reminder to the neighbours of their continuing presence.

A carnival for some, but many bereaved families found it difficult to rejoice.

The day of celebration was approaching, and the local MP, Mr Samuel Samuel, announced that he would give a plate and mug commemorating, as he put it, "The Great Victory of the British Empire" to every schoolchild in the constituency, an expansive proposal not uncommon at the time. The scheme however proved fraught with problems. First of all, the London County Council would not allow the pieces to be distributed in their schools. The reference to the MP's name, they said, gave the gesture a political overtone, a decision that irritated Joseph Davis to such an extent that he wrote to the *Wandsworth Borough News* from 94 Elsenham Street to voice his anger. Then the desperate shortage of coal meant that the manufacture of the souvenirs was heavily delayed; and they were not eventually handed out until October, by which time the moment had passed.

The peace committee had further worries. It had always planned that the local schoolteachers would act as marshals throughout the day, but the previous week they withdrew their support and refused to help. Their main point was that the children's activities should have been planned for during the week, in other words one of their own working days. Furthermore, the Southfields event coincided with the national day of celebration (and consequently a holiday for the many people who regularly worked on Saturdays) and they had rather hoped to spend the time with their own families. Urgent pleas went out for volunteers from the general public and many parents responded. It was also seen as an encouraging gesture that even a local councillor and his wife cancelled their plans to attend the main ceremonies in London and stayed with the Southfields children.

The day itself started fine and people made their way to the ecumenical service of thanksgiving held in the open air on the Wandsworth Technical School Sports Ground situated on the land north-east of the station. The ceremony started at 9 o'clock with an emotionally-charged rendition of the national anthem, and the collection at the end raised over £3 which was put towards the provision of a new cot at Putney Hospital. The ambitious scheme of decorations in the vicinity of the station was a source of great comment. The entrance itself was draped in crimson cloth, and banners were stretched across the roads bearing the names of the allies. Wreathes of laurel and other evergreens were everywhere. The railway bridge displayed the sober slogans, "Honour the Brave" and "In Loving Memory of the Fallen"; and the entire bill amounted to £4 1s 8d.

Just after midday, the procession itself set off from Southfields Station moving northwards towards Granville Road and Merton Road. The column consisted of brass bands, wounded ex-servicemen, staff from local firms, nurses, scouts and, most important of all, thousands of schoolchildren. G. Goodley &

Sons, the motor hauliers based at 15 Replingham Road loaned a fleet of six lorries to be used as floats, one of which carried a local character dressed as Charlie Chaplin who "evoked roars of laughter by his amusing antics".

The procession re-entered the Grid at Brookwood Road and made its way north up Heythorp Street and then round to the golf club. For the thousands lining the route, the high spot was without doubt the sight of the children. A journalist at the time reported:

> "(they) looked radiantly happy, and the air was rent with their shrill cheers as they wended their way through the gaily decorated streets. The girls, in their neat white summer dresses, presented a particularly charming appearance."

The carnival itself was attended by over 20,000 people. There were races, competitions and prizes galore; the one for the "best-decorated cycle" particularly captures the innocent exuberance of the time. Sgt-Major Eggelton of the Scots Guards drew a large crowd when he gave one of his well-known sword displays, during which he sliced a dead sheep in half with a single blow. The beast was then cut up and chops

Henry Parker's photograph of the Peace procession travelling westward past the junction of Trentham Street and Brookwood Road, with one of Goodley's Thornycroft lorries in the middle of the picture. The firm was much praised later in the year for the excellent service it provided transporting food during the protracted rail strike.

The editor accepted this advertisement for the March 1919 issue of the St Barnabas Church Magazine. *His readership was clearly more broadminded than we sometimes allow ourselves to believe.*

were given away as prizes in the somewhat tactlessly named "race for old ladies and men over 40".

The clouds were gathering by 4 o'clock when tea was served to over 5,500 children, and Mr Samuel talked to many of them as they munched through their little bags of fruit cake, a couple of buns and a quantity of toffees. He was no doubt determined to boost his local standing and get his money's worth. He did after all generously pick up the tab for their teas, and that amounted to £286 9s 2d.

At that point the skies opened and people scampered to the tents. In the largest marquee, where disabled soldiers from Roehampton Hospital were being entertained, Mr Samuel was delivering a speech, and the unfortunate gentleman had to suffer the indignity of bellowing in order to try and make himself heard above the din of voices. The poor chap could not even hold up one of his commemorative mugs in a silent gesture. So sadly the *al fresco* concert and the dancing on the green were cancelled as the bad weather set in for the rest of the evening. Yet in the face of so many setbacks and difficulties it really was truly remarkable that the day of celebration was any success at all.

That year like any other was a mixture of tragedy and joy. 66

Large crowds
gathered to watch the
inauguration of the
Southfields War
Memorial.

S. Barnabas' Church, Southfields.

FORM OF SERVICE

FOR THE

Blessing of a Calvary

✠

ERECTED IN PROUD
AND GRATEFUL
REMEMBRANCE OF
THE OFFICERS,
NON-COMMISSIONED
OFFICERS AND MEN
OF S. BARNABAS'
CHURCH AND DIS-
TRICT WHO FELL IN
THE GREAT WAR,
1914—1919.

BY THE RIGHT REVEREND

The Lord Bishop of Kingston-on-Thames

ON

SATURDAY, OCTOBER 4, 1919.

year old Samuel Bullock of 51 Astonville Street jumped off a moving bus at the end of Brookwood Road at the beginning of October and died from his injuries. During the previous month poor Clara Wheatley, a recent inmate of Brentwood Mental Hospital, committed suicide at the station, and the *Wandsworth Borough News* reported gruesomely that she had been "practically cut in half". Replingham Road was witness to a distressing incident on 27 September. Lily Gorton, who lived at No 93 was visiting her friend across the road. She was wearing a black and white dress made rather full and must have been standing too close to the fire. Horrified passers-by found her in the street, her frock in flames, and she later died of shock.

On a happier note, St Barnabas Church was the setting for a

pretty wedding on 12 July. Ivy Hockey of 141 Clonmore Street was married in ivory *crêpe-de-chine* with an orange blossom wreath. There was an exotic twist. Her husband lived and worked in Dunkwa, Gold Coast (now Ghana). Did they have a foreign honeymoon? Far from it! In an era of much narrower horizons than our own, they went to Folkestone.

Yet with the coming of peace, the community still had one final gesture to make. The idea of a memorial cross or Calvary had been mooted as long ago as the summer of 1918, and with the end of the war the need for some focus for grief had become quite urgent. Whitehead and Sons at Kennington Oval were commissioned to execute the project and a huge block of granite was cut at a quarry in Cornwall. Problems ensued. The original piece broke during carving, and delays were caused by government restrictions and the dire labour shortage.

Eventually the memorial arrived, quickly to be followed by the masons' bill for £240. The date for the unveiling was set for Saturday, 4 October 1919. The memorial bears the names of some 160 men from the district, irrespective of their creed, who died in the war and invitations were sent to all of their relatives. The ceremony of dedication at the corner of Merton Road and Lavenham Road started at 3.30, and many local residents without tickets pressed against the railings to watch the unveiling by Lieutenant-Colonel R. Hue-Williams. The Calvary was then blessed by the Bishop of Kingston and the service ended with the Last Post sounded by four buglers of the Coldstream Guards positioned on the roof of the church.

It had been a moving event, very trying for the bereaved, and Rev. J. Warren noted with relief, "Not a word of criticism has been offered about its design." He was curate-in-charge at the church, and his anxiety perhaps is a mark of a personality described by a contemporary as devoid of humour. He did though summarise his feelings that autumn with these touching remarks: "So there it stands - this beautiful representation of the supreme sacrifice, with its silent but eloquent appeal to all who pass by." For decades afterwards, the memorial has fulfilled its duty to act as a reminder to us all of that dreadful period.

Into the Jazz Age and Beyond

Steadily the warriors returned to a land far from fit for heroes. To ease the crushing effects of economic depression and heavy unemployment, Wandsworth Borough Council introduced a number of job creation schemes including the construction of a large park at the northern edge of Southfields. Confirmation that the opening would be performed by no lesser personages than King George V and Queen Mary lifted the event onto an entirely different plane. The original intention had been to call it Southfields Park, but now the area was to be named after the King and a source of exceptional civic pride; and Saturday, 28 July 1923 was set to be a day of major local celebration and great ceremony.

However the weather took a different point of view. The morning began with pitiless, driving rain and wind, and the conditions were so atrocious that the King personally telephoned the mayor from Buckingham Palace with the request that the expected 30,000 school-children and wounded ex-servicemen should stay under cover until he arrived. Sad to say it was still pouring as the royal car made its way into the park, though by then the thousands of children had taken up their positions on the rising ground near Buckhold Road.

The borough council secured the youngsters' enthusiastic loyalty by giving each of them a flag and a souvenir tin of Rowntree's chocolate bearing the portraits of the royal couple. Few of the specially printed programmes survived however; the rain put paid to that. There were large contingents of scouts and guides in the park, a common sight in the twenties when many churches such as St Barnabas formed huge troops as part of an expanding movement of youth activities. One such girl guide was Edith Robinson who lived in Gartmoor Gardens at the time. As the King walked past her group, he said to her, "I expect you think we are a nuisance keeping you waiting in all this rain." "No, Sir," she replied with well-rehearsed courtesy, "We came specially to see you."

Within a few minutes the sun had broken through the clouds

and the King and Queen were greeted with displays of very great affection. The *Wandsworth Borough News* reported that there was such waving and cheering "as had not been seen since the end of the war". Queen Mary in particular cut a truly dazzling figure. According to an exotic, hot-house description of the period, she was wearing an inevitable toque, silver in colour on this occasion, and "a dark blue wrap over a dark blue frock with iridescent embroideries". With her courtly inclinations of the head, *The Times* noted, "(she) never failed to leave proud and smiling recipients of her gracious and womanly notice."

One such recipient was Mrs Helen Pulleyn, mother of Lieutenant Pulleyn, the RFC officer who had been killed in the war. She was wearing his medals, a standard convention at the time, when she was noticed by Queen Mary who stopped to talk to her. Bursting with pride the *St Barnabas Parish Magazine* commented that the Queen leant forward, fingered the decorations and

Queen Mary in dark blue with a sequined toque talks to a wounded ex-service man at the opening of King George's Park in July 1923.

> "in a few kindly words expressed her sympathy as only a mother who has known suffering and bereavement could do."

Mrs Pulleyn remembered the moment for the rest of her life.

The calamities of two world wars act as book-ends enclosing the era of the twenties and thirties. So let us consider that period as a single unit, assessing in turn the influence of the local churches, home life and commerce before moving on to the impact of the cinema.

Throughout the nineteen-twenties, St Barnabas Church continued to exert its presence on the activities in the area. In 1922, it became the centre of a parish in its own right, and around the same time its old and dilapidated organ was replaced by one more fitting to this new status. The church's choir was large, typically 30 singers, and an anthem was included in most of the services. Its work in the community was complemented by the opening of the vast Wesleyan-Methodist Central Hall on Durnsford Road. Lady Holloway performed the ceremony on 24 September 1925 and its towering mass was to dominate the skyline until the early nineties. Despite a reference to Southfields in its popular name, the building was technically outside the area and stood in the former Borough of Wimbledon. For many years it was a centre for outstanding week-end concerts, and for enormous Sunday Schools drawing well over 1000 children a week.

A running social feature throughout the interwar years was the annual St Barnabas Summer Fete, held on a number of sites including the Durnsford Road Recreation Ground and from the mid-thirties in the grounds of the newly-completed Whitelands College. For a while in the twenties, it found its home in the large field adjoining George Bowman's house called Fernwood at the corner of Victoria Drive and Albert Drive. The festival in 1925 was a particularly successful event, blessed by "brilliant sunshine and the scent of freshly-mown hay". The organisers had chosen 4 July, and the merriment lasted for seven hours from three o'clock in the afternoon. The Metropolitan Police Band provided the music and there were prizes yet again for that sterling favourite, the best-decorated bicycle. Our old friend, Sergeant-Major Eggelton came over from Windsor and once more performed wonderful deeds with his set of swords.

A notable personality at the church during the twenties was the parishioner Kathleen Liddell, who left a lasting mark albeit after her death. She and her husband lived in substantial affluence at The Firs, one of the enormous villas on Inner Park Road. They were both active workers at St Barnabas and when she died, handsome oak panelling was installed around the altar in her memory. At the dedication on 30 October 1930, the Bishop of London spoke in fulsome praise:

> "She showed it was possible for a person to be a saint, and a pleasant and agreeable companion in one."

His Grace seemed to be hinting at some personal surprise over this apparent contradiction.

Clerics were meant to be austere moralists and disciplinarians in those days, and another example is provided by the vicar himself. Rev. Herbert Green held the post at St Barnabas from 1926 until the start of the Second World War and his notoriety

CHURCH OF S.BARNABAS

SOUTHFIELDS

⁂ PARISH MAGAZINE ⁂

No. 397	ONE PENNY.	MAY, 1937.

lingers on. Even now he is remembered as a very strict man not above hauling an errant choirboy out in front of the entire congregation, thereby generating high levels of embarrassment all round.

With the arrival of the nineteen-twenties, public transport was improving right across the capital, and Southfields was only one of the areas to feel the benefit as a consequence. Bus design was yet to change, and the fleets still looked similar to the sort that had carried troops to the front in the previous decade, complete with solid rubber tyres, open tops and outside staircases. From around 1923, the No 39 bus route began to carry passengers from Wandsworth Town Centre to Southfields Station, though not without its side effects. In September 1930, an infuriated Replingham Road resident

wrote to the *Wandsworth Borough News* to complain about the rate the buses tore along the roadway. "Are we to wait till the houses fall down round our ears?" he moaned; "They shake fearfully." His stress levels were not helped by the fact that he had to paper over the ceiling to cover up the cracks.

Those celebrating the opening of the new park in 1923 would not have been aware of it, but the cost of living in the area was to remain remarkably stable for many years to come. In the autumn of 1925, James and Agnes Brown redecorated two of their bedrooms at 127 Elsenham Street. Not only did they have electric light upstairs, they also had a bathroom; and this meant that the Browns could pitch their weekly rent at 15s or £1 for each of the rooms, depending on its size.

In 1930, the lodger at 81 Astonville Street was paying 18s a week. Six years later Victor Shackleton wanted 16s 6d for three unfurnished rooms at 105 Clonmore Street. "Adults preferred," he hinted. An advertiser in Engadine Street wasted no time with such subtlety in 1937. "No children" was the deal, if a newcomer wanted a first-floor flat with shared bathroom for 17s 6d a week.

There was a marked shift towards home ownership in the nineteen-thirties in line with a general housing boom in southern England. Here again though, the prices stayed

Southfields Station, c. 1924. The frontage has been remodelled, resulting in a wider public entrance and the removal of the large, glass lantern from the corner of the building.

reasonably steady. In April 1930 for example, Anthony Hoppe wanted to move from his home at 127 Lavenham Road and he offered it for sale at £550. Three months later, Jessie Mayersbach wanted £750 for 94 Heythorp Street, which she self-consciously described as a "pre-war house". At the other end of the decade, in the spring of 1939, the same price of £750 was sought for 18 Elsenham Street, and in the August of that year the slightly smaller 47 Elborough Street, an allegedly "much sought-after villa", was up for sale at £595.

The change to electricity was still very gradual however, and the street-lighter continued to play his part, turning on the gas-lamps as dusk began to fall. In 1935, Bob Bolton's father paid £6 to have electricity installed at 99 Heythorp Street, but only on the ground floor. The bedrooms were still lit by gas. Many older residents would not consider the change at all, even though the Electric Light Co. offered from 1937 to install the utility free-of-charge.

Amid this period of considerable stability, interesting changes were taking place in business, trade and culture. Branches of the chain stores were by now well established in Replingham Road: the shoe-shop Freeman, Hardy & Willis at No 13, United Dairies opposite at No 10, a small Co-op at No 42 and a Home & Colonial grocery store further down at No 73. In contrast, new independent arrivals included William Bourne who started trading as an ironmonger at No 30 in 1926, and Alfred Christmas who opened his chemist's shop at No 33 in 1932.

For a short while in the twenties, Cresswell's sold pianos and gramophones from No 16, mostly on hire purchase, while their neighbours at No 18, the long established chemists Enness & Co., did a roaring trade at Christmas time. Customers could buy perfumes in pretty boxes and all sorts of other toiletries for family gifts. Fortunately they could return a couple of weeks later if they wanted, because the shop also sold its own, very popular gout mixture. At this period of the year, the local paper confided, people who may be gouty usually find their ailment at its worst.

Further south on the Grid, Nicholas Hernig's story is of some interest. He set up as a baker and confectioner at 130 Brookwood Road and by 1935, he was so successful that he opened a second shop on Durnsford Road. "Families waited on daily," was his promise. But his own family origins were German and he fell victim to a bout of national hysteria at the start of the war. The authorities treated him as an enemy alien, and he spent the bulk of his time in an internment camp in the north of England.

His was only one of a staggering number of shops in the area at the time. In 1936, the count along Brookwood Road was something like 44, with a further eight in the more residential Lavenham Road. At the end of Brookwood Road, Wynn's Ltd. established a small bottling plant in 1928 where they made fizzy drinks. In that same year George Mason opened his OK Sauce factory at 265 Merton Road (now the site of Autocue House) and the spicy aroma it produced went on to pervade the nearby streets for the next 41 years. In marked contrast, pigs were kept at Dunsford Farm which was situated further south at the eastern end of Brookwood Road. When the wind was in the wrong direction, the smell was so pungent that people often had to close their windows. As if that was not enough, Ernest Cleverly did a roaring trade in manure at the corner of Merton Road and Revelstoke Road, from where he kindly offered to deliver it onto local gardens for a shilling a bag.

A final note on one of the other professional personalities of the time, albeit from a very different walk of life. Mian Mohammed Shaffi set up his practice as a doctor at 69 Replingham Road in the years between the wars. Here was a community quite untutored in multi-culturalism, and his dark presence was seen as strange, if not slightly intimidating. He is nevertheless remembered for saving at least one person's life.

The intellectual side of things received a boost with the opening of a library in 1934. The former builder, William Castle, was by then a counsellor, and he had worked hard for many years to get such a facility established in the area. The proposals had been more than a decade in the pipeline and when the library did finally open on 18 June, it was greeted with a certain amount of grumbling. If the residents had expected custom-built premises like the ones in Earlsfield, they were in for a disappointment; it was a small, converted sweetshop at 21 Replingham Road. Still at least it was modern, and it was set up on the lines of an "open access" self-selection system.

In his opening speech, Councillor Castle picked up on this feeling that the area had been fobbed off. With uncanny foresight he said that he would have liked to have seen a noble building on Wimbledon Park Road. "Perhaps that will come in the future," he added. At least he had no doubt about its target market: bored housewives. "Most of the workers (in the area) have occupations in the City," he pronounced, "but now their wives will have no more lonely moments"; and at a stroke we have an insight which confirms our worst fears of how things used to be.

The cinema developed into the main form of popular entertainment in the nineteen-twenties, and the middle of the decade is often seen as the heyday of the great silent-movie stars. The Lyceum followed closely in step with that trend, changing its programmes twice each week and offering top quality films often within a fortnight of their general release.

Taken at random during that silent era, the synopses of a couple of pictures shown during the week of 5 October 1925 read like a parody of the whole genre.

> Mrs Wallace Reid played a mother in "Broken Laws" who unquestioningly tries to protect her reckless son after he becomes involved in a fatal car crash. A manslaughter charge follows, his father threatens severe punishments, and it is only during the court case, amid a wild and hysterical appeal, that she awakens to her own folly.

> In "A Sainted Devil", Rudolf Valentino appeared as Don Alonzo de Castro, a young south American of fortune. On the night of their wedding, his bride, the beautiful Juliette, is forcibly abducted by the bandit, El Tigre. Our hero swears revenge.

The prices were always easily affordable and ranged between 3d and 1s, to which a small entertainment tax was added. Live musical accompaniment was a regular feature from the start and in the early days, it was provided by the well-respected Excelsior Orchestra.

Technology advanced rapidly, and by 1929 suburban exhibitors were in a state of transition. Some films were still completely silent; others were described as "part talkie". By the end of the following year, "Singing, Talking, Dancing" pictures were a regular feature, some even described as "Entirely in Natural Colour", though to our well-tutored eyes it would not have looked like the sort of colour that nature ever intended.

On Armistice Day in November 1930, the Lyceum showed the film "Journey's End", a version of R. C. Sheriff's anti-war play and considered at the time: "the greatest of all talkies". It drew large audiences and was a rarity for Hollywood; there were no women in the cast. The Lyceum management were in controlling mode and reacted accordingly:

> "Patrons are reminded that to gain the maximum enjoyment from this film it is necessary to be seated before the film commences."

But in due time, the old building started to look its age. In June 1936 it closed for refurbishment under the direction of a young architect, Richard Seifert, later to win notoriety for his design of Centre Point in New Oxford Street. The management changed the cinema's name and started an intense publicity campaign. "Watch it grow!" they urged. "Start saying Plaza." The old facade was entirely remodelled, and all the seats were replaced so that the audience could sit in great comfort and watch programmes lasting up to an amazing three hours, still outstanding value with seat prices ranging from a mere 6d to 1s 6d. Patrons to the renovated cinema were reminded of the free parking facilities, which was a nice way of saying: "Leave your car in Pirbright Road."

On 29 June, the mayor, Councillor John Keall, braved the heavy rain to perform the opening ceremony and Henry Parker who ran a photography business at 106 Brookwood Road took the picture for the local paper, a conflicting image of dinner-jackets, afternoon frocks and a little girl looking startlingly like Shirley Temple. The opening speeches betrayed a certain self-consciousness. "I will not admit that Southfields is the

The Mayor of Wandsworth, Councillor John Keall, buys the first ticket at the Plaza Cinema on its opening night in June 1936.

Cinderella of the borough," confided his Worship. "There is no need to go to London to see the pictures now," added Councillor Castle who pops up yet again in the area's story. However this impression of second best was not entirely dispelled by the choice for opening night, a lacklustre programme of "Charlie Chan in Shanghai" and Laurel and Hardy's "The Bohemian Girl". A local critic enthused: "the two funsters have many opportunities of displaying their inimitable style of pantomime," which possibly explains the film's subsequent drift into oblivion.

An amateur talent contest was held every Friday evening at the Plaza from the middle of January 1937. There were tap dancers, lady saxophonists and Mr Warner, the facial contortionist, though now we can only hazard a guess at the range and quality of these entertainments. But to help us, here is a selection of comments from that first spring:

"The singing was strongly rendered."

"(The performer) crooned to some purpose."

"Miss Cullum made her concertina "talk"."

"Miss Hedger wound up briskly with her accordion."

One evening the manager, Charles Banks, "told an amusing story of what happened when two butlers took their respective masters' bulldogs for a walk up Park Lane", though after the passing of so much time, we will have to fill in the punch-line for ourselves.

The two concepts of tradition and Empire run strongly through this entire period. On the side of tradition, that early dairyman, William Skinner, had grown into a well-known character of great antiquity. He had moved to 368 Merton Road, and received an invitation to go to Buckingham Palace in 1929 as part of the Police Centenary celebrations. By then he was 94, and he was granted a privileged place amongst the special seats, since he was believed to be the oldest living policeman at the time.

Seven years later one famous event occurred which was seen as symbolising the passing of another age. On an unforgettable night at the very end of November 1936, crowds of people made their way up Augustus Road. Standing in groups, they looked back in sorrow to watch the flames from the old Crystal Palace as they leaped high into the sky.

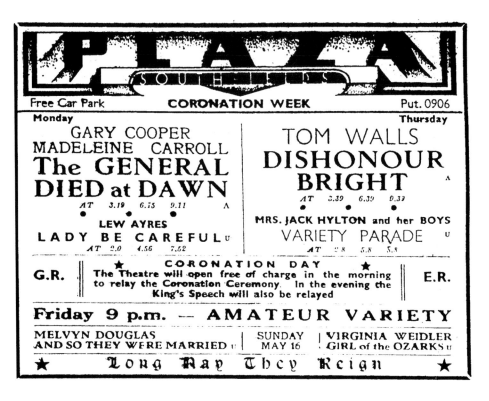

On the subject of imperial loyalty, one of the distinguishing features of that St Barnabas Fete in the summer of 1925 was the involvement of many children from the schools on Merton Road in the performance of a "Pageant of Empire". Patriotic displays were the standard routine each year on 24 May, which had been Queen Victoria's birthday and was widely observed as Empire Day. Speaking at Riversdale School in 1930, Rev. Green gave a "homely and pithy" speech which generally reflected the dutiful if patronising sentiments of the great majority of his audience's parents. In essence he argued that there were two sorts of pride in the Empire: one which was mere flag-waving and bombast, and the other, more worthy kind which meant a sense of responsibility for all British people.

Only a week earlier, George Gale had been slightly injured at the corner of Astonville Street and Brookwood Road. He was the son of Beltran Gale, the sewing-machine dealer at 195 Replingham Road. Clearly something of a gilded youth, he had a miraculous escape when his car collided with a 30 cwt. lorry. "To the amazement of eye witnesses he was apparently unhurt," they said. Most interesting in the context of the time is the fact that he was a well-known member

Coronation week, 1937 – the Plaza Cinema uses contemporary graphics in the heading to its advertisement, but plays it safe when it comes to the rest of the layout.

51

of the Junior Imperial League, which is perhaps best described as a forerunner of the Young Conservatives.

Loyal fervour reached its peak in the mid-thirties with the Silver Jubilee of King George V in May 1935 and the Coronation of King George VI two years later. Street parties had been so successful during the Jubilee that they were revived for 1937 with renewed eagerness, though the rain which marred the whole of Coronation week meant that most had to be held indoors.

Empire Day, by now renamed Commonwealth Day, was brought forward to 11 May for that year and the mayor, William Heath, visited the schools on Merton Road, enchanting the children with his scarlet robes of office and with the mace-bearer who accompanied him. With the mayoress, Alderman Heath distributed some of the borough's souvenir spoons, a standard design decorated with the royal portraits which set the budget-conscious council back by less than 9d each.

Albert Cleverly, the wireless dealer at 15 Replingham Road, fitted up loudspeakers at Riversdale School so that all the speeches could be easily heard. It was a time for cautious satisfaction, and this inspired the mayor to say that with all the unrest in the world, Britain remained at peace as her industry increased and unemployment decreased. Yet the reality was still enormously distressing for many. Only two months earlier, 26 year old Ernest Pavely, whose family ran their model-aircraft business from a tiny, dark shop at 187 Replingham Road, had taken a fatal overdose while suffering from depression owing to his lack of work.

On 12 May, Coronation Day itself, Southfields scouts were up before 6 o'clock and detailed to act as programme sellers in Green Park. Local school-children joined 37,000 other youngsters in a special section on the Embankment to watch the procession, and 12 year old Kenneth Hext of 124 Trentham Street actually sang in the abbey choir during the service, receiving the King's silver Coronation medal for his efforts.

Interest was so intense that a newsreel of the ceremonial was shown at the Plaza just two days later on the Friday. Before the end of the month, local boy scouts held a rally at St Michael's Playing Field, where they performed such exotica as flag-pole erecting at speed, trek-cart races and a jungle dance. Eli Slatter of 123 Heythorp Street composed a song, "A Coronation for Two" and sent a miniature copy to Princess Elizabeth for use in her dolls' house. Patrons who attended the amateur talent competition at the Plaza on 21 May had the good fortune to hear him perform the very number itself. Mr Slatter, it will be recalled, also wrote that other forgotten favourite, "Tweet! Tweet!".

However those with more sensitive ears were already picking up a different tune, as they watched Wandsworth Borough Council getting their preliminary Air Raid Precautions into place. In May 1937, it asked for volunteer rover scouts to act as despatch riders if other lines of communication were to break down, and minds were further focused when an exhibition opened on 2 July with demonstrations on how to put on a gas mask and how to make a house gas proof.

A way of life was drawing to its close, and with just weeks to spare before the coming of war itself, the old order of things dealt the Grid, almost literally, one final blow. On 23 May 1939, Queen Mary paid a visit to the Royal Horticultural Gardens at Wisley. The fateful decision was made that she should return home via the route she regularly used after watching the tennis at Wimbledon. Her maroon Daimler had just made its stately way past Southfields Station and was travelling up Wimbledon Park Road when it was struck at the junction of West Hill Road by a lorry carrying a load of steel piping. The limousine was overturned and all five occupants were badly hurt. Some nearby workmen ran to the spot and they extricated the injured with the help of a couple of ladders.

The Queen and her staff were taken to the house of Dr Stanley Revell at 44 West Hill Road, a GP who had held a surgery for many years at 2 Elsenham Street, earning enormous respect from his many patients. However by some sad stroke of fortune, the good doctor had died the previous week, but the injured were nevertheless tended by his son Frederick, who bandaged the lady-in-waiting's arm and was complimented by the Queen on the neat job he had made of it. To the Queen herself he gave a refreshing cup of tea and an aspirin, as well as a copy of the newspaper reporting his father's death. Hitting just the right note, she asked if she could keep it.

The lorry driver was also very shocked but otherwise unhurt. He later sent a bouquet of flowers and a message of sympathy to Marlborough House, though the reaction of his insurance company to that gesture is unrecorded.

Eventually a replacement car arrived and according to *The Times*, the large crowd which had gathered "showed their relief and sympathy in a burst of cheering", which the Queen acknowledged with a composed bow. Even the worsening European situation made its impact on the incident. Among that crowd was Fraulein Frizi Adler, a refugee from recently occupied Czechoslovakia. She told a local reporter, "I have been here only ten days and I did not know she was a Queen, but she looked one."

The whole incident was exceedingly distressing to Queen Mary. By then she was 71 years old, and her contained dignity was severely ruffled. King George and Queen Elizabeth were in Canada on their influential tour and could not easily be contacted, and the injury to her eye would trouble her for the rest of her life.

She was confined to bed for ten days, and the maxim Heads Must Roll came into play. Within a week a three-day traffic census was set up on what became known as Queen Mary's Corner, and there were demands to install a set of traffic lights. This was something of an over-reaction since the survey revealed that only 180 cars passed the spot in any one hour. At a meeting of the Highways Committee the following month, a certain Alderman Mills made his views plain when he pointedly remarked, "If proper care had been taken by both drivers, the accident would not have occurred." So we find that as the world teetered on the very brink of catastrophe, at least one councillor was quite untouched by any reverence for his betters.

War Yet Again

The start of the Second World War is such a dramatic moment in history that it seems reasonable to suppose that its arrival one bright, Sunday morning was an event which nobody was expecting. In fact the reality disproves this assumption, and the preparations were clearly apparent to the people of south London well before the beginning of September 1939. There were those ARP demonstrations in 1937 for instance, and in 1938, the old and less than fragrant Dunsford Farm on Merton Road was demolished to make way for an anti-aircraft battery and Territorial Army barracks (now the home of the 31st Signal Regiment).

This unnerving heading appeared in May 1939, nearly four months before the actual outbreak of war. Albert Cleverly traded in Replingham Road from 1934 until 1969.

On a Sunday in May 1939, the authorities set up an ARP exercise in Wandsworth which involved scattering 150 tennis balls within the space of half an hour, each one representing a single bomb. The following week, a parade of ARP workers, firemen and St John's Ambulance members marched from Southfields Station to St Michael's Church in a show of reassurance to the thousands in the area who would soon be so reliant on their services. By the time that war was declared, offices had been set up at 42 Replingham Road to act as a base for enrolling ARP personnel and for distributing their equipment.

Gas masks were handed out in early June. Anderson shelters were delivered to homes in the same month and immediately became an essential feature. When 120 Heythorp Street was put on the market in the autumn at a rent of 30s a week, the advertiser was keen to confirm to his readers that a shelter was already in place in the back garden.

The blackout, soon to be a source of great frustration for the next five years, was tested over south-east England on 10 August and the papers reported that there had been "a good response". It was nonetheless an eerie experience. As travellers waited at their bus-

stops the lights disappeared all of a sudden, a moment which many found both unnerving and disorientating.

For Britain, the opening phase of the conflict was marked by the Phoney War when the civilians stood and waited, not knowing for certain what to expect. Not much seemed to be happening. The children who had been evacuated for safety returned home. Ration books appeared in mid-November, and shoppers queued up to register with their chosen grocer. The World's Stores was still going strong and it easily attracted its fair share of loyal customers. First-class tickets were withdrawn from the District Line but still there was no drama to concentrate the mind.

The spring and early summer of 1940 saw little change on the home front, though the news from the continent grew

Flora Beaumont stands bravely at the entrance to her Anderson shelter in the back garden of 11 Trentham Street, c. 1940.

increasingly grim. However Croydon Aerodrome was bombed in August, and the sound of the explosions could be heard across the whole of south London. Finally in September, the east end of London suffered its first bombing raids. Southfields no longer needed a reminder that it was at war, and its impact fully struck home on 11 September when 89 Astonville Street was hit by a high explosive bomb which was described at the time as an "aerial torpedo". No-one was killed but scores of people lost their homes, and severe cracks appeared in the western wall of St Barnabas Church.

Among the wardens on duty that night were Kenneth Braidwood of 114 Engadine Street and Bert Potty of 126 Lavenham Road. Mr Potty in particular was a popular character, though people had poked a certain amount of fun at him during the monotonous tedium of the Phoney War. In the event when put to the test, he came up trumps and was much praised for carrying on, despite suffering from shock as a result of the explosion.

Not all the victims were human. During the course of the following day, a well cared-for tabby-cat turned up at St Barnabas Vicarage demanding hospitality in no uncertain terms. Not surprisingly the poor thing was such a bundle of nerves that nothing would induce it to come indoors.

In a flash everything had changed. The pupils of the Elliott School were gathered together and hastily moved out to Guildford; while the Methodist Central Hall provided temporary shelter for the families made homeless by the Astonville Street bomb. The Luftwaffe aimed at the railway line and hit Elsenham Street time and again: No 42 on 15 October and No's 173, 176 and 142 on 29 October, though the latter bomb failed to explode. It rained heavily the following morning, and a very bedraggled and sad-looking police officer could be seen standing guard outside the house, awaiting the arrival of the bomb disposal squad. In the days that followed, residents consoled themselves with the thought that German dissidents were bravely sabotaging the things in their production factories and rendering them harmless.

More destruction had been suffered a week earlier when houses in Revelstoke Road were badly damaged on the 20th by a high explosive bomb which landed at the top end of Braemar Avenue. The severity of the air-raids brought home the intensity of the war; and so did the incidents of friendly fire, when anti-aircraft shells burst in Clonmore Street and

A static water tank in the playground of Merton Road School offers an emergency supply source if the mains are fractured during an air-raid, c. 1940. Across the road, Stacy's Acmé Laundry has obliterated the "Southfields" from its fascia panel in an attempt to create confusion if enemy forces invade the area.

Elborough Street. Civilian morale could have easily collapsed with disastrous consequences if there had not been a feeling of unshakeable resolve to resist the enemy. Central to this was the discipline of the ARP workers. The Grid was defined as area D.30 and the Post Warden in charge was Alfred Claisse who lived at 156 Elsenham Street. He in particular is the man we must thank for co-ordinating the efforts of the other wardens in the surrounding streets and for conscientiously building up a record of the many incidents which occurred during the following four years.

The Engadine Street Fire Squad came in for special praise that winter. They had been organised to tackle the increasing problems caused by falling incendiaries and their captain was Joe Tringham of 174 Revelstoke Road who worked out of Tom Hendra's shop at No 126 (now Butt's the Newsagents). For the most part he was supported by two wardens, James Le Brocq of 136 Engadine Street and Joseph Goodchild who lived across the road at No 137. Together they organised a rota of about a dozen householders who took it in turns to watch each night and bang on a dustbin lid whenever they needed to raise the alarm. If that did not call for sufficient courage Alfred Houghton of No 154 was especially applauded for his great determination. He had sent his wife and two children away to safety in Wales where, by some hideous stroke of irony, they were all killed when their shelter received a direct hit during an air-raid.

May Ellen still has strong memories of those war-time fire-raids. She recalls one night staring out at the scene from an upstairs window, and looking down on a complete semi-circle of fires, an experience which she describes as "horrid". The following morning she found an empty canister in Heythorp Street with words in German on its side, the chalk lettering still sharp and white, and looking for all the world as though they had been written only a few moments earlier.

These utterly abnormal conditions posed a number of acute moral dilemmas. A conscientious church-going public needed guidance on how to conduct themselves if their service was disrupted by the sirens. There would be a short pause, they were informed at the start of the blitz, during which the choir-boys would leave; and then the service would recommence for those who wished to stay behind. There was yet another concern that must have caused some of the more fastidious parishioners considerable personal dismay. Could you consider yourself dispensed from fasting from midnight before communion if you were involved in overnight war-work? The new vicar at St Barnabas, Rev. Joshua Speechly, ducked the issue, it has to be said, when he urged people to search their own consciences on the matter. He did however add with stirring resolve:

> "Above all, the enemy must not drive us from the things that matter most - the practice of our religion."

What of the day-to-day recollections from that period? Long-standing residents remember shifting quickly into a regular routine: home from work - on with the oldest slacks - into the Anderson shelter. But the shelters soon flooded, and many people made the conscious decision to sleep under the stairs instead. Better to risk bomb-blast than a bout of bronchitis! The nights were nerve-wracking experiences of droning enemy aircraft and loud bangs from the anti-aircraft guns at the TA Headquarters nearby. Private emotions swung between despair and a frustrating lack of information. There was a desperate shortage of accurate local news, since only vague details of the bombing appeared in the papers. The naming of roads could prove of vital value to the enemy, the censors argued.

During the days following the heavier raids, the youngsters who had stayed behind ran around the streets collecting shrapnel and other pieces of bomb casing. Sometimes they set up a small display to collect money for charity. Petrol became scarce, then impossible to obtain; and Joyce Weller talks of a large, green Rover motor-car which sat for many years in splendid isolation beside the kerb in Heythorp Street, only to disappear as if by magic within days of victory.

Saving for the war effort became a full-time occupation. In August 1940 the mayor, William Bonney, organised a Spitfire Fund with a view to the borough raising money for as many fighter planes as it could afford. The collection proved so successful that Wandsworth eventually presented three. The Spitfire nominally linked to the Putney, Roehampton and Southfields Parliamentary Division was commissioned in January 1943 and finally written off as unserviceable on 10 May 1945.

St Barnabas Church set up an ingenious fund-raising scheme that lasted throughout the war, whereby parishioners were asked to donate all their pennies dating from Queen Victoria's reign to pay for repairs to the church organ. Clearly not every activity was directed solely towards the prosecution of the war, even though the parish was surrounded by so much strife.

The rhythm of life carried on, of course: births, deaths and marriages. Typical of many war-time weddings was the one celebrated on 17 March 1941. In a local match Sgt Thomas Brown of 160 Clonmore Street was married to Barbara Davis of 84 Heythorp Street. Owing to the clothing shortage, the bride was not in white, but wore instead a blue-green two-piece suit with a spray of anemones to match. Yet a glimpse of opulence still managed to surface. When she left for their honeymoon, it was an ocelot fur coat that she wore to cover her navy-blue costume.

Bravery was honoured that month when Acting-Sgt Observer Robert Pavely received the Distinguished Flying Medal from the King at Buckingham Palace. He was a relative of poor Ernest who had died in 1937, and he had lived for many years with his uncle, Douglas, helping in the design and manufacture of model aircraft. The experience proved invaluable during his reconnaissance work over Germany with the RAF. His machine was attacked on one such trip. It caught fire and yet he was able to bring the plane safely back to Britain.

Eventually the nightly air-raids ended in May 1941, and the war started to move in a subtly different direction. Rev. Speechly wrote excitedly in the July of his great relief that the two greatest dictatorships were at last in conflict. As a clear indicator of this changing situation, he could take the risk of holding a garden party that month at the vicarage.

The old and greatly under-used train link from Southfields to Waterloo was quietly withdrawn during the spring, but few people noticed. They had more than enough to occupy their time. In their zeal for self-sufficiency and home-grown food, they turned over part of Wimbledon Park to allotments once again, and most householders converted their gardens into little farms. Chickens provided eggs, and lawns made way for potatoes, beetroots and other staple crops. There was however a problem: they all came up at the same time, creating a minor feast-and-famine syndrome.

With increased enthusiasm to pursue the war to a successful finish, a series of salvage drives came into full swing. Kitchen waste could be converted into animal food-stuffs, and scraps of metal into planes and bullets. In a decision of far-reaching impact, the Ministry of Works and Supply set about the removal of all garden railings in the summer of 1941. The men arrived out of the blue and rapidly sawed them off, leaving behind their stubble remains as a reminder to this day. The railings were stored for a long while, which gave the impression that they were never used for any such purpose. In fact, the metal was re-cycled, but only slowly and over an extended period of time.

There was much excitement among church-goers that September with the receipt of reassuring news from behind the enemy lines. Rev. Spencer Gerhold had come to St Barnabas as a member of the clergy in 1930 and he lived with his mother at 160 Heythorp Street until November 1935. He moved to a position on Guernsey and remained there when the Nazis invaded in 1940. News eventually filtered out the following year that he was well and carrying on his work, though he was later deported by the occupation forces. After the war he returned to the island where he remained until his death in 1969, a stalwart of the local Boy Scouts Association.

There followed years of drab tedium and food shortages, but "hit and run" attacks had arrived by early 1944 and local residents once again faced the constant fear of losing their homes. On the night of 24 February, 129-133 Replingham Road were destroyed and a shower of incendiaries started fires in the area around St Barnabas Church. A full container of incendiaries blew out the front of 388 Merton Road, and an empty one crashed down on 159 Brookwood Road. When it was announced that Mr Collett of 1 Elborough Street had been killed in the attacks, the news was received with widespread sadness.

Members of the Home Guard march past Southfields Station on an overcast morning, c.1944.

The first appearance of the flying-bombs in the summer was greeted with elation; with all those flames angrily spitting out at the back it had to be an enemy plane that our gunners had shot down. Such wishful thinking was quickly forgotten in the days that followed. Mercifully no V1's fell on the Grid though wherever they landed (as happened on Stuart Road and twice to the east of Replingham Road), blast damage extended over a very wide area.

Progress to victory was clearly being made, although it was sometimes hard to feel convinced of the fact while unmanned rockets continued to fall onto London from out of the skies. Nevertheless after five years of blackout, the regulations were finally eased and half-lighting was introduced on 17 September 1944. People at home were allowed to cover their windows with nothing thicker than their peace-time curtains, and side-street lighting was also restored. They nicknamed it the "dim-out" and the citizens of Wandsworth were urged to donate to the RAF Benevolent Fund in thanksgiving.

Here are three more news stories to capture the flavour of 1944 - tales of dry humour, pride and tragedy tinged with recklessness. In the August, Walter Wiseman and his wife celebrated their 60th wedding anniversary at 100 Trentham Street. He was a little taken aback when a reporter asked if any of his family were in the forces. "Lord, no!" he chuckled. "They're too old! They were in the Great War!"

Four months later in December, Mr and Mrs Noble Britton of 154 Brookwood Road went to Buckingham Palace to see their son, Dennis, receive the Distinguished Flying Cross. He had flown more than 50 times over occupied Europe on pathfinder missions. At the end of the same month, the burial service of Flt Sgt Eric Sweeting of 10 Elborough Street was held at St Barnabas, his coffin draped in the Union Jack. Earlier in the war he had lost his commission for a low-flying prank whilst instructing some American pilots. During the ceremony, a member of the congregation sang one of his favourite pieces, "I Know That My Redeemer Liveth." He was so young that he did not even have the vote when war was declared.

Unlike 1918, the end of the fighting in Europe in 1945 came as no great surprise. People had been expecting an announcement for days; only its timing was a matter for debate. By 7 May the country knew that the following morning would see the arrival of VE Day, and decorations started to appear spontaneously in the streets. On the Grid there was hardly a house without a flag. At 31 Replingham Road, Charles Thorp decorated his cake-shop with all the allied flags and "masses of people" came to look at the display, according to the *Wandsworth Borough News.*

VE Night itself was a pleasant, warm evening with women in summer dresses and men strolling about in their shirt-sleeves. It felt more like a bank holiday and a large congregation assembled at St Barnabas amid an unforgettable atmosphere of

Albert Cleverly showed great commercial flair and regularly placed advertisements on the front page of the Wandsworth Borough News. *He directly influenced their design and text, and they were generally different in each issue of the paper. This advertisement appeared on 20 April 1945, two-and-a-half weeks before VE day.*

thanksgiving and heartfelt relief. They united to sing "Praise My Soul the King of Heaven" before returning to the streets where by now most of the Grid was out enjoying itself. Bonfires were lit in this mood of heady celebration only to be abandoned in the small hours to burn themselves out. True to form the grumblers had a field day, complaining later that the fires had made a lot of smoke and noise, and that many invalids had been unable to sleep. It is always valuable to have the mind soberly refocused even in moments of harmless exuberance.

There followed a series of street parties which lasted many weeks. By coincidence Saturday, 12 May was the eighth anniversary of the Coronation and festivities were arranged to equal that earlier celebration. Typical of many was the party organised by Lillian Bonner for the children of Elsenham Street. She booked the Methodist Central Hall on Durnsford Road and planned five hours of festivities. A few oranges were found, and a little ice cream and glasses of fruit cordial were also served. William Austin from 111 Elsenham Street sang and played the piano. One of his neighbours took along to the hall his radiogram, the forties' equivalent of a sound system, which added substantially to the cheery mood of the afternoon.

Victory had been achieved in Europe; yet Japan remained an implacable enemy. There was a general feeling that the struggle would continue for a long time to come, with the result that the Japanese surrender on 14 August, after the dropping of two atomic bombs, caught many people by surprise. One of the many who was greatly disturbed by the news was Rev. Speechly. He was a man whom Eddie King described as "a splendid vicar", though he is remembered by others, mostly children at the time, as chilly and firm. In the September 1945 issue of the *St Barnabas Parish Magazine*, he put down on paper his troubled thoughts about this appalling new method of destruction:

> "We are probably all too near the shock of this thing to make a sound, final judgement. (It) makes it impossible for me to lead you in any act of joyful thanksgiving…for the victory over Japan."

Others came to terms more quickly with such moral quandaries and prepared to rejoice at the return of world peace. One feature of the Wandsworth celebrations was the distribution once again of a commemorative tea-spoon. Its design was full of symbolism and pulled together a selection of suitable motifs: the sword of mercy, a pair of doves and the highly emotive letter "V". The borough's name and 1945 were proudly stamped in the bowl and one was handed to every child in the area.

The other mark of celebration was the organisation of "the biggest garden party ever", designed to last over two days. This event arose from an idea put forward by William Heath who had visited the nearby schools in 1937 when he was mayor. He owned "Ravenswood", a large house near Holy Trinity Church on West Hill (inevitably converted into flats in 1954), and he generously offered the use of his grounds for the party.

Wednesday, 19 September was the date allocated to the residents of Southfields and admission was free. Everything was in short supply: crockery, staff, even envelopes. Indeed the paper shortage was so dire that the invitation to all the local school-children took the form of an advertisement in the *Wandsworth Borough News*. Visitors were promised "really good amusements", including six little ponies, an unrideable horse and "a topping little roundabout"; and 7,000 people took up the offer on that day alone. Getting them there was a problem and anyone with a car was asked to volunteer to shuttle the children from Southfields Station, for which they received a special windscreen sticker and a small allocation of coupons from the Petroleum Board.

The atmosphere at the party was tremendous, largely due to the dynamic energy of Alderman Heath himself. At one point he called out to the children, "Are you having a good time?" "Yes!" they replied with a deafening roar, and their cheering lasted for many seconds. At another stage he took hold of a microphone and led the crowd in a rousing rendition of "God Save the King".

Posterity was not forgotten either. The whole event was recorded by the Ministry of Information Colonial Film Unit for distribution to an anticipated audience of 60 million people throughout the Empire. In this manner a momentous chapter in local history drew to its close. Peace brought reconstruction and the task of restoring the bomb sites. Late forties' doors and window-frames and the small blocks of post-war flats are clearly visible to us today, tributes perhaps to those who held fast and lived through such a period of harrowing uncertainty.

Post-War Memories

During the first years of peace, there were around 55 businesses in Replingham Road and a further 37 in Brookwood Road. The vast majority were independent concerns supplying the day-to-day food and service needs of a small, modestly comfortable community which in its turn was typical of many similar suburbs right across the country. Let us try and capture the flavour of this era, based on the reminiscences of a number of older residents, without feeling too heavily burdened by the discipline of any specific dates.

February 1958 – the arrival of Independent Television meant that brands such as Sunblest bread were much better known to the general public.

Interestingly, certain smells still linger strongly in their memories. For example, James Mitchell ran a small cooked-meat shop at 20 Replingham Road, so tiny that the presence of three customers would fill it to capacity, and other shoppers had to queue outside on the pavement. Passers-by could pick up the smell of boiled ham way down the road. All slices were cut by hand, and a request for as little as two ounces was quite acceptable.

Further up at No 12, Spicer's Stores always had the aroma of firewood and fire-lighters about the place. Frederick Lickfold sold wet fish at No 6, and each morning he would open up the front of his shop so that passers-by could inspect the cod and haddock lying on his cold slabs.

Miller's the Bakers traded next door at No 8, which has been the location for a bread-shop without a break since the premises were first occupied by Alfred Spells in 1903. Mr Miller did a roaring trade, though frequently, it has to be said, his loaves smelt slightly burnt. By way of contrast, mention Nicholas Hernig, in business at 130 Brookwood Road once again after his years of internment as an enemy alien, and memories

MILLER'S OPEN SOUTHFIELDS' NEW SUNBLEST BAKERS SHOP!

OPENING DAY
FRIDAY 14th FEBRUARY

Miller's announce they will open a new Sunblest bakers shop on Friday 14th, at 8, Replingham Road, Southfields, S.W.18.

Hours of business from 8 a.m. to 5.30 p.m. daily.

Oven-fresh goods delivered three times a day.

AND Miller's invite you to come and see the special display of wedding and celebration cakes!

Miller's have branches in Wandsworth and Putney High Streets, and throughout Tooting and Balham.

LOOK FOR:

★ A wide variety of Sunblest bread, plain and fancy, *and fresh to the last slice.*

★ A full range of "crusty" breads.

★ An excellent selection of cakes and pastries at popular prices.

66

of the wonderful smell of his bread still bring gasps of admiration.

Further along the same road at No 106, Henry Parker continued his reign as the principal photographer in the district. During the war he was under a government contract to make a photographic record of military machinery and various bomb-sites. He possessed a powerful singing voice which was a source of pride to him. There was, however, one minor drawback. It was so awful that only the bravest of his friends ever asked for an encore of his "Here Comes the Galloping Major".

Life was not easy for many of these traders. Mrs Hillyer, who ran the other fish shop on the Grid at 60 Brookwood Road, would regularly go off to Billingsgate Market at five in the morning, only to return with her stock just as groups of children were making their way to school. Such levels of commitment were quite usual at the time.

Other businesses led an unchallenged existence, generally operating in the face of little competition and creating for themselves an unassailable niche in the affections of their customers. One such could be found at 25 Replingham Road where Miss Seldon functioned as a corn-dealer, following in her father's footsteps and setting out on the pavement each morning her sacks of lentils, beans and chicken feed.

This sense of continuity meant that incongruous glimpses of pre-war glamour could still be found, even in the drab years of late-forties austerity. In an age with different clothing tastes from our own, Mrs Edgar Bell of 100 Lavenham Road described herself in the *Post Office London Directory* as a "furrier". In addition, there flourished at 5 Replingham Road a café run by the suavely named Auguste Giraud. His sliced French apple tarts are remembered to this day, and his fortunate location was the making of a minor success story. Wimbledon Tennis had been revived in 1946 after a pause of seven years, and those first post-war championships were attended once again by large crowds of spectators. His was one of the few places at the time where they could buy any decent refreshments, a situation which turned his little business for two weeks of the year into a veritable gold-mine.

Further down the road at No 43, Mrs K. Lambert traded under the name of Mary Quality and sold patterns, needlework kits and made-up cushions. She was well known for her charity work and collected huge quantities of silver paper in support of guide-dogs. On the same side of the road, the long established Madame Edythe soldiered on as a milliner at No 85. She had started as a blouse manufacturer during the First World War and survived until the late sixties when ill health forced her to retire.

Many businesses still employed delivery boys whose duties were not only to keep the shop fronts tidy, but also to walk around the streets supplying their many customers with fresh produce such as loaves of bread from their large baskets, or fish from a small barrow or cart. From time to time these youths would cross the paths of various milk-floats which were still drawn by horses well into the late fifties. Competition was strong amongst the dairies, and newcomers to the Grid were often delighted to receive one week's free milk in a bid to attract their long-term custom.

Generally speaking, profits were never high, and some of the smaller, privately owned shops struggled hard to make ends meet. As a result, they often put off the expense of converting to electricity. Many were still lit by gas into the early fifties, which made them seem particularly dark in winter time. London continued to suffer from bouts of dense fog, and flares would blaze at street corners on especially bad evenings as people struggled to make their way home in the impenetrable gloom. Dustcarts were still horse-drawn until as late as 1956, and it was often sad to see them slipping and straining during winter time, as they tried to get a grip on the icy streets. A more pleasant experience at other times of the year was the appearance of a borough water cart, sprinkling the streets and laying the dust. They left an air of freshness whenever they passed by.

The Plaza remained a thriving source of entertainment though the fuel shortages in the war often meant that it had been very cold and uncomfortable. Nevertheless, returning servicemen and their families packed the place out on Friday and Saturday evenings. One glimmer of refinement survived; patrons could order tea during the Saturday afternoon performances.

Local youngsters developed their own method of cost control. One of their group would buy a ticket and get into the cinema. He or she would then leave an emergency exit ajar and the others would "bunk in" from the back. Contrary to the impression they formed during those visits, being a cinema manager was far from glamorous. You can watch a film only so many times before tedium sets in, and the Plaza's manager overcame his boredom by regularly taking out a stock of books from the library in order to while away the long hours ahead of him.

The Plaza's fortunes began to wane in the fifties. Its red plush seats grew increasingly lumpy and unyielding, and an altogether different group of patrons started to make up its audience. As the LCC flats were completed on the nearby estates, so their tenants, many of them arriving from as far as Bow, took up occupation in their new homes. Tensions were felt; and at times the welcome they received was equalled only by the warmth of their own enthusiasm. To put it bluntly, many of the newcomers did not particularly want to be relocated in the first place, and resented the dislocation they had experienced. Their initial presence at the cinema sent a startling message to some of its longer standing customers, who linked its subsequent decline directly to their arrival.

These reminiscences began with the sense of smell; let them end with the sense of sound. Long forgotten is the presence of music in the streets: the cries of the muffin men and the songs of the buskers. Every Sunday, the Salvation Army held their services at various street corners, filling the nearby houses with the strains from their band. In the same vein, the appearance of the Boys' Brigade was always a source of great excitement. Along the streets they would march, complete with drums and bugles, and their tuneful passing never failed to draw groups of people to their front doors.

A New Era Dawns

Life was definitely getting easier. By the start of the fifties, the days of austerity were practically over, and more and more families were experiencing new levels of prosperity. As mentioned in the previous chapter, new blocks of flats were beginning to rise near the Grid, changing the horizon to the west out of all recognition, while the value of existing properties steadily increased year by year. At the lower end of the scale for example, John Reed put 96 Lavenham Road on the market in October 1953 for £1,795, at a time when other houses were fetching between £2,200 and £2,800.

It was a period of significant political change. The Conservatives, with Winston Churchill at their head, swept back into power after a six-year experiment under Labour. A young princess set forth for Africa and, amid great sadness, returned only a few days later a queen. After a four month gap, Garter King of Arms proclaimed that Tuesday, 2 June 1953 would be the date of her Coronation, and arrangements gathered momentum for a truly exceptional year of festivities.

February 1953, and Albert Cleverly is already whipping up interest in the event of the year.

70

By the following spring those plans had come to fruition. Henry Vivian of 53 Clonmore Street decided to mark the occasion by obtaining council permission to purchase and plant two rows of trees along the middle section of his road. On 30 May, a pageant and fayre took place on the playing fields at Viewfield Road. Local schoolchildren sang and danced *en masse*, and Jean Marshall appeared as a charming Gloriana in a wistful tableau which harked back to the previous Elizabethan era.

The Skeena Hill Allotments and Gardens Association held a Southfields Coronation Front Garden Competition for all the enthusiasts in the area. Window boxes were excluded, and entrants were assessed on, among other things, an "absence of weeds". That particular June saw record rainfall and the judges were compelled to tramp round the streets in their soggy macintoshes before they could announce the results. The Grid, it must be noted, failed to figure among the winners.

Coronation morning was a scene of great activity at 158 Elsenham Street as Lawrence Pottle prepared for his journey up to central London. The 17-year old was a corporal in the Boys' Brigade and he had won a place lining the route near Buckingham Palace. He got pretty wet before the end of the day. As TV viewers right across the country switched on their sets at 10.15, they were greeted with scenes of rain-swept roadways and sodden uniforms.

But television lifted the event into another world, and it was no surprise to Albert Cleverly that a large crowd gathered both inside his shop and on the pavement in front of 15 and 17 Replingham Road to watch the events as they happened on a bank of black-and-white screens.

The day proved to be a moving experience which united the vast majority of the population in a quite extraordinary manner. People were surprised by the fact that their already high hopes had actually been surpassed, and Rev. Speechly neatly caught this feeling when he wrote:

> "Like, I suspect, most of you, I was far more deeply impressed by the Coronation than my best expectations had led me to suppose. For this, in part, one has to thank the BBC for the wonderful arrangements both for sound and television."

Such was the continuing level of emotion, the management of the Plaza could present without embarrassment "A Queen is

Crowned", the Technicolor documentary scripted by Christopher Fry, more than a full month later on 5 July.

By then, the Grid had seen a host of organised parties. In Engadine Street, Walter Clements brought out a sheet of tarpaulin from No 92 and this was stretched over the tables in the form of a tent to protect the crowd of 60 children from the rain. Lavenham Road held their event at St Barnabas Hall in Acuba Road and each child was given a cardboard crown to wear instead of the usual party hat.

Notable among the others, Trentham Street held their festivities at Riversdale Primary School, attended by the local MP, Sir Hugh Linstead. He had been knighted in the Coronation honours list and he presented the prizes together with his wife, Alice. At least some things never seemed to alter. Amongst the competitions an old favourite turned up yet again: the best decorated cycle!

A Routemaster bus starts its return journey in this evocative photograph of Replingham Road, dated 27 September 1956.

1956 saw further change. The Elliott School, so long established on the east side of Merton Road, moved to a new site in Putney, and William Castle's dream of a purpose-built library came to fruition two decades after he first publicly

72

expressed it. On 10 October, the Mayor of Wandsworth, Mrs Olive Haines, travelled to Southfields to perform the opening ceremony in Wimbledon Park Road amid a good deal of local pride. The architecture of the building was commended for its balance of spaciousness against the low cost of its construction. Furthermore, the library could boast about being the first lending counter in the country designed for a new method of issuing books known as "photo charging".

The church still exerted a strong influence on many people's lives, and so it was hardly surprising that St Barnabas should once again become a focus for sad reflection. John Stroud had joined the congregation in 1911. In the years that followed he became a churchwarden and later a lay-reader. He was the Mayor of Wimbledon from 1950 to 1952, and after his death the next year, Marlborough Road (just north of Ryfold Road) was re-named in his memory. On 12 June 1957, a ceremony to his memory was held in the Lady Chapel at the church to consecrate two altar-rails made by local craftsmen. On the same occasion, a "corporate memorial window", designed by Marion Grant, was also dedicated. In former times, a single family used to finance the installation of an entire stained-glass window, but by the middle of the twentieth century, such an idea was simply too expensive to contemplate. Under this new scheme a family could sponsor an individual panel and allow space for others to follow, though it comes as no surprise to note that none appear to have been added since the window's first appearance.

In the spring of 1958, the *St Barnabas Parish Magazine* asked, "Is Doreen dated?" Three Doreens had been married in the church during 1957, but the name had not appeared on a single occasion in the baptismal register during the same period. A community that worries about such things cannot be altogether bad.

Yet there were indeed a number of worries to tax people's attention. Hylda Willis of 39 Lavenham Road was so irritated by door-to-door salesmen offering anything from disinfectant to paraffin heaters that she planned to put up a "No hawkers" sign. But coal by then was no longer readily tolerated because of the killer smogs it had caused, and the creation of a smokeless zone under the Clean Air Act of 1956 forced householders to make a choice about switching to coke, gas or some other form of cleaner fuel. Consequently those heaters that were such an annoyance to Mrs Willis would have found an eager welcome in some other quarters at least.

Southfields Station, c. 1954, with the Plaza Cinema's façade on the right. The large sign over the station entrance still refers to the Southern Railway, though the company had ceased to exist following rail nationalization in 1948.

The Replingham Road shopping centre still retained its semi-rural feel and managed to close for half a day on Thursday afternoons; yet there was an appreciable build up in the volume of traffic. In February 1958, Albert and Louisa Munn echoed the anxieties of many of the older residents. They had married in 1908 when Southfields was, according to their description, "like a country village lit by gas lamps." They lived at 20 Heythorp Street till the late thirties when they moved to 39 Skeena Hill. To them the junction outside the station had become a danger spot, both bewildering and frightening, and they felt sure that it needed a zebra crossing. They did not have to wait long; traffic lights were installed early in 1959.

Increasing exasperation over the train service started to bubble to the surface. Congestion had steadily grown over the years with the arrival of the new housing estates, and a campaign demanding improvements gained ground in 1956, only to be forced to take a back seat during the Suez Crisis. But by early 1958, anger had mounted once again. People nicknamed the Wimbledon branch "the Cinderella line", and they complained that the carriages were "disgustingly full". They bewailed the fact that they had to suffer an inadequate service south of Putney Bridge which amounted to only four trains an hour, even during the normal times of the day.

The Wandsworth Ratepayers' Association moaned about the discomforts, delays and frustrations of their suburban journeys. "We travel just like cattle," they said, and they raised a petition with 2,700 signatures on it, backing a campaign for the revival of the old service to Waterloo. This found little favour with a certain Mr Hart of the LCC, who sharply replied that such a proposal would be uneconomic. The volume of traffic would be insufficient justification, he said, and in his opinion, only Southfields and Wimbledon Park would benefit. Many years were to pass before a truly acceptable level of service was finally provided.

There was one final surprise to trouble these otherwise tranquil years; quite without warning the Plaza closed in October 1957. It may well have seen better days, but the cinema was still treated as a place for family entertainment, and it was widely appreciated for all that. For a few weeks the letters column of the *Wandsworth Borough News* was filled with agitation. With such a population increase in the surrounding area, one correspondent wrote, the place should surely be better attended. Another added that, despite the lure of TV, which was scornfully dismissed as a "peep show", the wonderful films of the day were all in colour. They got their wish. The cinema re-opened as part of the Essoldo group at the end of March 1958 with that robust British epic, "The Bridge on the River Kwai".

Harold Macmillan told the British public that they had "never had it so good" and, as the fifties made way for the next decade, increasing affluence meant that there were more jobs than people to fill them. A feel for the period is gained by the following local vacancies advertised in 1963 by the Southfields Secretarial and Employment Bureau at 2 Replingham Road:

- Short-hand Typist, aged 19-20 at £9 per week

- Male Clerk (Grammar School Type) for Planning Dept. at £14 per week

- Personal Assistant, aged 22-28 at £725 per year plus luncheon vouchers

Without knowing it, we were losing our innocence; and that process of maturity led to the deeper social and economic changes of the Swinging Sixties. Barclaycard arrived in 1966, a bright symbol of the evolution in shopping habits taking place right across the country, and this new confidence and prosperity was bound to have an impact on an area such as Southfields. Not surprisingly, most of the shoe repairers had closed since the end of the war, and the last remaining watchmaker had also gone, but hairdressing salons were on the increase. The one at 83 Replingham Road called "Jules", a name so evocative of the radio programme "Round the Horne", has a particularly exotic ring to it.

A pet-shop replaced one of the dairies and a couple of bookmakers had arrived, reflecting the changes in the law governing betting. TV repair shops were catering for another new need, while Albert Cleverly battled on to the very end, eventually going into retirement in 1969 after 35 years in the business. In 1966, he was still advertising confidently on the front page of the *Wandsworth Borough News*, with an encouraging call to watch the World Cup, in black-and-white of course, on a new push-button 19-inch TV set. The rental charge was a modest 8s 9d per week.

This survey should not close without a passing nod to one of the more bizarre commercial ventures in the area's entire history. The borough's *Official Guide* for 1967 carried a full write-up about Starboard Marine, a sailors' chandlery operating out of 56 Brookwood Road. The account explained that the firm was:

> "formed in 1956 by a yachtsman who, with years of cruising behind him, wished to supply yachtsmen with their needs and beginners with welcome advice."

At last the hidden sea of Southfields had found its way onto the nation's navigation charts.

Property values rose steadily in the sixties and houses on the Grid were being advertised in January 1968 at prices ranging from £5,650 to £5,950. Alert to the need to satisfy the ever-growing demand for modern housing, Wandsworth Borough Council cautiously agreed to the demolition of a row of hundred-year-old houses on Merton Road, replaced them with the small estate called Hanford Close. Practically opposite that development, the new Southfields Comprehensive School was nearing completion, at a construction cost of about £800,000, and destined to include a "furnished model flat" as part of its domestic training unit for senior girls.

The local churches reflected the main world issue of the day and set up earnest charitable collections for the relief of refugees fleeing the war in Vietnam. It was anniversary time at St Barnabas and the vicar, Rev. Jack Clark, celebrated the church's diamond jubilee in May 1968 by taking approximately 100 people on a pilgrimage to Canterbury. The large turn-out was no surprise, since the deal was a good one. The price was set at just 12s 6d - and that included afternoon tea.

Yet there was one final event which indicated that local life was turning a corner. During the week of 5 January 1968, Lynn Redgrave appeared in "Georgy Girl" at the Plaza, after which the screen went blank for the last time. The management had finally to bow to the inevitable, and yet somehow they succeeded in re-inventing themselves. By mid-May, Essoldo Bingo announced that they were "due to open shortly". They advertised for callers, which is understandable, but they were also seeking to recruit "stewardesses". Perhaps after all, Starboard Marine had greater influence than we first imagined.

The Oaks Finally Mature

The talking points on the Grid a quarter of a century ago clearly show when we entered the era we know today. The signs are plain to see. Quite simply, the worries that caused most trouble then are the same ones that dominate our lives now. In essence, these are housing problems, the issue of parking and securing decent public transport.

Take housing first. By the mid-seventies there was a real concern that the area would deteriorate beyond all recognition. A major survey was undertaken by the borough's Planning and Transport Committee in the autumn of 1976 with the aim of sorting out various local problems. Using the political jargon of the day, they set up a consultative "think tank" involving the Southfields Grid Residents' Association and the Southfields Small Properties Tenants' Association, and it came up with some significant findings. Just under half of the properties on the Grid were rented unfurnished; that is to say, people paying a weekly or monthly rent to the owner. This was obvious in many of the streets, where the landlords used to paint whole rows of front doors in the same colour.

Many of the houses which were actually owned by the occupier had not been modernised and these were simply wearing out. Well over 10% of the total had no inside toilet, and up to a third lacked the basic amenities such as a bathroom. Many people made do with a gas-fired heater in the kitchen to provide all the hot water they needed. A large number of the householders were elderly, some having settled on the Grid during its early years and, sixty years later, they were often living alone. It was estimated at the time that the proportion of people living in Southfield Ward and drawing a pension was about 18%. (By 1996, the figure had dropped to nearer 13%.)

As these older occupants died, the pressure increased to convert their family-sized houses into flats, and it looked extremely likely that the whole area would lose its appeal to families of three to five people. In contrast it would become more suitable for singles or couples on short-term tenancies and, so the story went, the charm of the Grid would be shattered for ever by a new type of population which felt no long-term loyalty or affection for the community in which it lived.

In the event disaster was averted. The building societies became increasingly reluctant to offer mortgages on conversions at about the same time as the council decided to call a halt to the trend and review its planning policy. Instead it toughened its resolve to preserve much of the character of the neighbourhood and save it as an essentially residential area. It may have recognised the changes in shopping patterns and tolerated the many conversions from shops to offices, but it redoubled its efforts to publicise its housing improvement grants which encouraged the installation of more inside toilets. The living areas in the houses were taking on a different feel too. Originally they had been a set of little rooms; now the fashion was well established to open up the downstairs and "knock through", in order to create more space.

Not everyone, of course, was enchanted by the district. The ultimate author of that survey in 1976 was Michael Tapsell (who was to die six years later following a heart transplant), and he fretted about the lack of community centres and open space, and the fact that the roads were regularly used as short cuts. He added:

> "(The) houses are generally well maintained, (but) the continuous criss-cross pattern of the streets makes the area rather monotonous."

Ignoring such anxieties, property prices steadily increased and by the spring of 1978, people were speaking in shocked terms of houses in Brookwood Road going for £16,950 and in Trentham Street for £19,950. Two decades later, ten-fold increases on those figures were taken as a matter of course.

The problem of parking remains a divisive and apparently insoluble irritant. In 1958, there were rarely more than three private vehicles to a block and yet twenty years later, the streets had become almost imperceptibly burdened with cars. The suburb was ill-prepared to cope with such an onslaught. The original developers had made no provision for such things - but then, how could they? The existence of such monsters was quite unknown to them. The problem lies in the sheer density of the population coupled with its increasing affluence, and one of the prime virtues of the Grid - a general friendliness borne out of living in closely packed Edwardian terraces - has turned into a shortcoming. That council survey of 1976 expressed growing fears about the parking problems near the station. It found that 47% of households had a car. (This contrasts with the Putney Traffic Plan of 1997, which can be assumed to reflect a reasonably reliable picture for Southfields. There the authors reckoned that 75% of households owned at least one car, and that 22% of the total owned two.)

Nevertheless the surveyors could still propose an ingenious plan to ease the difficulty of cleaning the streets, a suggestion that would be considered laughable today. On nominated street-cleaning days, the residents would be asked to park on one side of the road only. Failing that, a controlled parking zone scheme was about to be introduced in Putney. Its initial success would be closely monitored and a similar arrangement might be introduced into Southfields at a later date. There's no such thing as a new idea...

Public transport had been exasperating since the very beginnings, but there had never been such demands on its resources as were being felt by the mid-seventies. The majority of residents still did not own a car and people grumbled that the No 39 bus service was notoriously unreliable. Indeed the extension of its route in 1973 to cover the post-war housing developments around Augustus Road and Beaumont Road had only aggravated the problem, as did the constant shortage of spare parts to repair the buses themselves.

Nevertheless the Underground service had its moments of glamour. In 1973, passengers joining a train at Southfields occasionally found that they were sitting alongside an artiste of world renown - none other than Miss Marlene Dietrich. She was staying in central London for a short while and playing at Wimbledon Theatre. The tube was much quicker than road transport, she told people at the time.

The local electoral boundaries were reorganised in 1978, creating a Southfield Ward now with three councillors and sending out a clear message about the growth and needs of the local population. The SGRA actively lobbied for an improvement in public transport and spent the spring of that year gathering signatures for a petition to the Greater London Council. In the case of the District Line, they criticised the antique rolling-stock, and drew attention to the fact that the number of trains was quite inadequate for the increasing demand. You bought an 80p single ticket to the West End, they pointed out, and yet you had to wait up to 20 minutes during the off-peak period, double that time if there was a cancellation.

The trains themselves did improve, and by January 1980 a new style, known as "D Stock", was running on the City line and replacing carriages that had been built nearly 45 years earlier. They brought new comforts with them - single doors operated by passengers to retain the heat in colder weather. A final blessing arrived in 1984, to the general approval of many people. Smoking was banned and within weeks most travellers could scarcely conceive of a time when it had ever been tolerated.

Now is perhaps the appropriate time to introduce yet another personality into our story and relate her to the origins of the SGRA itself. By the start of 1973, a local resident, Mrs Tina Thompson, had sensed a need to draw together the energies and enthusiasm of various neighbours who were keen to serve their local community. She called a meeting at Southfields School, and out of those discussions the Residents' Association was born, an organisation which continues to fulfil its original objectives right down to the present day.

By 1976, Mrs Thompson had developed the idea of the Southfields Festival, a sort of village fete, and she became a prime mover and shaker in getting it under way. (The local girl made good. In May 1997, Councillor Thompson achieved the distinction of becoming the Mayor of Wandsworth for a year.) Fashions change, of course, and the event shrank to a shadow of its former self, finally coming to a halt in 1998. Yet the descriptions of the Festival in its heyday read more like King Edward's Coronation than anything we might arrange in our own time. In 1978, for instance, schoolchildren danced round the maypole while their parents judged the best bottle of home-made wine. Music came from the Southfields Concert Band, excitement from rides on a Young's brewery dray, and jollity from Rhubarb the Clown. Fortunes change and the Festival has been revived in 2000 to celebrate the millennium. The ghost of Rhubarb walks again!

Once again it was anniversary time at St Barnabas and the church, always proud of its "high church" reputation right from the start, decided to hold a Festival Eucharist in May 1978. As 70 years earlier, the preacher was the holder of the office of Lord Bishop of Southwark, "his entry heralded by a stirring fanfare", the *Parish Magazine* breathlessly reported. By now the Grid had acquired a sense of its own history, which accounted for the success of the "Southfields Seventy" exhibition. Old drawers were pulled open, scrap-books were checked and a wealth of nostalgic material surfaced for inclusion in the various displays. Newspaper cuttings, leaflets, printed scarves, photos, ration books; visitors were startled by the heritage revealed by the exhibits.

Looking back is fine in small doses, but present issues also require attention. The aggression of Idi Amin in East Africa, and the arrival of large numbers of immigrants, caused widespread anxiety in Britain at the time. A group of college students in Twickenham chose the Grid and its surroundings to research the problems of what they termed the "coloured community". Their report for the Wandsworth Borough Council for Community Relations was published in November 1978 and there is an unavoidable irony in their opening remarks which read like the writings of intrepid European explorers a hundred years earlier. As they walked around the streets they noticed:

> "(The houses) are mostly well looked after by the owner occupiers…(we formed) first impressions of the residents being friendly and convivial, evincing a sense of neighbourliness."

They had hoped to see more youth clubs and school classes on African and Asian cultures; but they applauded the enterprising attitude of the increasing number of Asian shopkeepers. The students nevertheless feared a "major race problem" in the future, and expressed their apprehensions in these terms:

> "Whether or not the present immigrant community (can) remain immune from racial strife elsewhere in the borough or in outside areas is an interesting speculation."

It must be said that a sincere tolerance and a general mellowing of feelings over time have rendered those worries generally unfounded.

Locations which had featured earlier in this history came back into focus in the nineteen-eighties. The old site next to the station, formerly used as the Technical College Sports Ground, was sold for the private development of about 50 houses and these were finally completed in 1982. The Essoldo Bingo Club, previously the Plaza Cinema, eventually closed in 1987, only to re-open later in the year as Jesters Snooker Club.

Southfields Library was also feeling the strain after 30 years of constant use and temporarily closed for refurbishment in September 1989. The books were transported up the road to Southfields Baptist Church until the work was completed over a year later. On 22 November 1990, the local MP, the Rt. Hon. David Mellor (who was also the Minister for the Arts at the time), performed the opening ceremony in the new, light-filled foyer.

He returned five years later to perform a similar function at the station, the ownership of which had transferred from British Rail to London Transport in April 1994. All through the eighties the buildings had deteriorated owing to vandalism and graffiti. The waiting room and toilets were permanently closed in 1987 but greater action was needed for security reasons and in order to cope with even larger numbers of passengers. And so it came about that David Mellor performed the necessary honours on 7 September 1995 standing in the redesigned entrance hall under newly upgraded strip-lighting and in the presence of closed-circuit TV.

New technology was affecting home life too. Contractors appeared on the scene in August 1994 and promptly dug up all the pavements, laying Videotron cables and providing a new utility for probably the first time since the arrival of electricity. There were shouts of annoyance at the level of disruption and great concern over damage to the tree-roots; but the installation teams soon left, though in truth their legacy has yet to fulfil its potential.

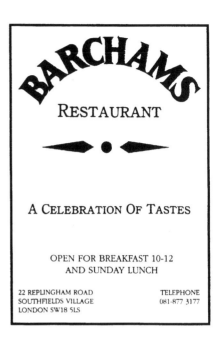

BARCHAMS

RESTAURANT

◆ ● ◆

A CELEBRATION OF TASTES

OPEN FOR BREAKFAST 10-12
AND SUNDAY LUNCH

22 REPLINGHAM ROAD   TELEPHONE
SOUTHFIELDS VILLAGE   081-877 3177
LONDON SW18 5LS

The short-lived Barchams Restaurant hints at continued rustic charm with its reference to Southfields Village in this advertisement from April 1991.

Finally one long-standing barrier collapsed with the arrival of the first pub on the Grid. The generally held belief that the whole area was somehow "owned by the church" is hard to confirm, and any remaining covenants are now clearly unenforceable. In 1994, J. D. Weatherspoon's purchased the building on the north-west corner of Heythorp Street, the site of the short-lived Bartram's Restaurant, and set to work on its conversion, settling on "The Grid Inn" for its name. All was complete by 6 October when the managers, Tony and Jenny Murly, opened the doors to their new customers. There was no music, a no-smoking area and the first guest ale was Deakin's Royal Stag.

The following summer saw plans to convert Jesters Snooker Club into a superpub. These were greeted with waves of local protest and the council refused planning permission in the November. But the ball was rolling and in 1997, the pub owners Greene King took over Brett Motor Services on Replingham Road and set about the construction of an "ale

It may have won an award in 1995, but Brett Motor Service said its good-byes two years later to make way for "The Old Garage" ale café.

café". Amid a publicity campaign on Kiss FM, "The Old Garage" opened for business during that mournful week following the death of Princess Diana and struggled against heavy odds and a violent stabbing before it found its way into the affections of the local residents. Quality of life had been challenged and was found to be precious.

And so a new millennium approached and with it an opportunity to celebrate the past and contemplate the future. Sensing the moment, the SGRA organised the installation of a commemorative signpost outside Southfields Station, and the mayor, Councillor Chief Lola Ayonrinde, visited the spot to perform the inauguration ceremony on 21 December 1999. The station still retains its function as the local point of reference and continues to display that commemorative shield with its bold date - 1889 - which reminds us of a momentous June morning in the latter years of Queen Victoria's reign. The olive-green engine has long since vanished, with its driver and its little wooden carriages. Also gone is the first train-load of railway passengers. But if by some magic they could all come back again and visit our shops, walk around our streets and enter our homes, what in the name of heaven would they make of it all!

Postscript

Reading this story, some might feel a sense of sadness. The passing of time has created an image of Southfields Grid as an Arcadian idyll adjoining meadows and hay-fields, its residents eternally content, whose only source of stress was the wide variety of shops, each concentrating on its own trade. Then came two world wars and expanding urban development. One-by-one those precious corner businesses closed and the ground floors were converted into offices or houses. Nowadays only the moulded corbels between the former facias at first floor level distinguish the buildings and hint at their earlier history.

But this sense of loss is decidedly misplaced. The Grid is less than six miles from the middle of London, and yet it still manages to weave its distinctive spell; against all the odds a charming impression of *rus in urbe* survives about the place right down to the present day. The area remains a profusion of trees providing shelter for foxes and squirrels, a mixed blessing as they invade our gardens and disturb our precious plantings. Added to this, there can be few more moving sights on a summer evening than a squadron of Canada geese flying back to base at Wimbledon Park, beating the air with their flapping wings.

Even the retail trade shows some encouraging signs of renewal. With the arrival of Boots the Chemists in June 1997, a chain store returns to remind us of many similar enterprises in earlier years. In addition the modest affluence in the area has sustained an exceptional selection of specialist food shops and restaurants that is hard to equal.

The only certainty is change and further developments are bound to follow; but as a century turns, we are forced to speculate on what will be left in another hundred years' time. Will these present houses survive that long? Will they be gentrified - or will the whole area return to dust, and come up for redevelopment in a form that we can scarcely imagine?

One Doomsday scenario has already been put forward, though it brings with it certain charms. What would be the long-term effect of another major oil-crisis? Would we enjoy the development of top quality public transport, as a time returns when only three private cars are ever seen on any one kerbside and the wistfully remembered corner shop of old comes into its own once again? Those change-of-use flats and offices may have a restricted shelf-life after all.

We all owe a debt of thanks to our predecessors. Our greatest challenge is to demonstrate our commitment to pass on the area where we live in a fine state to our successors. May they feel as grateful towards us as we certainly do to those who lived there in the years long past.

PRINCIPAL SOURCES AND FURTHER READING

Bailey, Keith *The "Grid": A Building History* (unpublished manuscript) n.d. (c1986)

Besant, Walter *London - South of the Thames* 1912 pp228-9

Borough of Wandsworth Official Guide 1967

Catling, Simon *The Changing Face of Southfields* 1978

Connor, Piers *Going Green - The Story of the District Line* 1993

Daily Chronicle 10 July 1912

Day, John R. *The Story of London's Underground* 1963

Heath, William *Peace Celebrations for Putney, Roehampton and Southfields* 1945

Kelly's Directory of Wandsworth (The "Buff Book") Selected issues

King, Eddie *Rambling Reminiscences* (unpublished manuscript) 1990

Knight, Donald R. *The Exhibitions - Great White City* 1978 pp18-9

Lee, Charles E. *100 Years of the District* 1968

MacRobert, S. *The Development of Putney* (unpublished manuscript) 1971

Metropolitan Borough of Wandsworth Official Guide 1956

Pope-Hennessy, James *Queen Mary 1867-1953* 1959 pp594-5

Post Office London Directory Selected issues

Punch 23 April 1930 pp467-8

Rondeau, Bernard *Wimbledon Park - From Private Park to Residential Suburb* 1995

Smith, Rebecca *The Geographical Change in a London Suburb: SOUTHFIELDS* (unpublished manuscript) n.d. (c1982)

St Barnabas Church (Parish) Magazine Selected issues

The Times 30 July 1923, 24 May 1939 et seq. & 25 March 1953

Wandsworth Borough News Selected issues

Wandsworth Historian Summer 1986 p13, Summer 1988 pp1-3, Summer 1992 pp10-13 & Autumn 1997 pp15-21

Wandsworth, London Borough of *Report by the Director of Planning on Southfields District* 1977

West London Institute of Higher Education *Southfields - A Report for Wandsworth Council for Community Relations* 1978

Wimbledon Borough News 21&28 Aug 1953 & 7 June 1957

Index

Page numbers in *italics* refer to the illustrations